Lecture Notes in Computer Science 14288

Founding Editors

Gerhard Goos

Juris Hartmanis

Editorial Board Members

The series Lecture Notes in Computer Science (LNCS), including its subseries Lecture Notes in Artificial Intelligence (LNAI) and Lecture Notes in Bioinformatics (LNBI), has established itself as a medium for the publication of new developments in computer science and information technology research, teaching, and education.

LNCS enjoys close cooperation with the computer science R & D community, the series counts many renowned academics among its volume editors and paper authors, and collaborates with prestigious societies. Its mission is to serve this international community by providing an invaluable service, mainly focused on the publication of conference and workshop proceedings and postproceedings. LNCS commenced publication in 1973.

Jelmer M. Wolterink · David Svoboda ·
Can Zhao · Virginia Fernandez
Editors

Simulation and Synthesis in Medical Imaging

8th International Workshop, SASHIMI 2023
Held in Conjunction with MICCAI 2023
Vancouver, BC, Canada, October 8, 2023
Proceedings

Springer

Editors
Jelmer M. Wolterink ⓘ
University of Twente
Enschede, The Netherlands

David Svoboda ⓘ
Masaryk University
Brno, Czech Republic

Can Zhao ⓘ
Nvidia
Redmond, WA, USA

Virginia Fernandez ⓘ
King's College London
London, UK

ISSN 0302-9743 ISSN 1611-3349 (electronic)
Lecture Notes in Computer Science
ISBN 978-3-031-44688-7 ISBN 978-3-031-44689-4 (eBook)
https://doi.org/10.1007/978-3-031-44689-4

This Springer imprint is published by the registered company Springer Nature Switzerland AG
The registered company address is: Gewerbestrasse 11, 6330 Cham, Switzerland

Paper in this product is recyclable.

Preface

The 8th Simulation and Synthesis in Medical Imaging (SASHIMI) workshop was successfully organized in conjunction with the 26th International Conference on Medical Image Computing and Computer Assisted Intervention (MICCAI) in Vancouver, Canada, on October 8, 2023.

A total of 16 submissions were received after a call for papers. Each submission underwent a double-blind review by members of the Program Committee (PC), experts in the field of simulation and synthesis of (bio) medical images. Each PC member reviewed, on average, three papers, and each paper was reviewed by at least three reviewers. After review, the PC chairs accepted 13 papers for publication in SASHIMI 2023.

The accepted papers span a wide range of topics relevant to SASHIMI and reflect exciting recent developments in methods for segmentation, image-to-image translation, super-resolution, and image synthesis. Applications include MRI imaging, echocardiography, PET, and digital pathology.

For the first time ever, SASHIMI was organized jointly with a challenge. The SynthRAD 2023 challenge aimed to provide a platform offering public data evaluation metrics to compare the latest developments in synthetic CT generation methods. The methods, results, and winners of the SynthRAD 2023 challenge were presented at the SASHIMI workshop event.

October 2023

Jelmer M. Wolterink
David Svoboda
Can Zhao
Virginia Fernandez

Organization

Program Committee Chairs

Jelmer M. Wolterink	University of Twente, The Netherlands
David Svoboda	Masaryk University, Czech Republic
Can Zhao	Nvidia, USA
Virginia Fernandez	King's College London, UK

Program Committee

Ninon Burgos	CNRS - Paris Brain Institute, France
Aaron Carass	Johns Hopkins University, USA
Blake Dewey	Johns Hopkins University, USA
Florian Dubost	Google, USA
Virginia Fernandez	King's College London, UK
Qian Ke	Bloomberg L.P., USA
Yuexiang Li	Guangxi Medical University, China
Anirban Mukhopadhyay	Technische Universität Darmstadt, Germany
Cattalyya Nuengsigkapian	Google, USA
Dzung Pham	Uniformed Services University of the Health Sciences, USA
David Svoboda	Masaryk University, Czech Republic
François Varray	Université Lyon 1, France
David Wiesner	Masaryk University, Czech Republic
Jelmer M. Wolterink	University of Twente, The Netherlands
Yuan Xue	Johns Hopkins University, USA
Heran Yang	Xi'an Jiaotong University, China
Can Zhao	Nvidia, USA

Contents

Transformers for CT Reconstruction from Monoplanar and Biplanar Radiographs

Firas Khader[1]([✉]), Gustav Müller-Franzes[1], Tianyu Han[2], Sven Nebelung[1], Christiane Kuhl[1], Johannes Stegmaier[3], and Daniel Truhn[1]

[1] Department of Diagnostic and Interventional Radiology, University Hospital Aachen, Aachen, Germany
fkhader@ukaachen.de
[2] Physics of Molecular Imaging Systems, Experimental Molecular Imaging, RWTH Aachen University, Aachen, Germany
[3] Institute of Imaging and Computer Vision, RWTH Aachen University, Aachen, Germany

Abstract. Computed Tomography (CT) scans provide detailed and accurate information of internal structures in the body. They are constructed by sending x-rays through the body from different directions and combining this information into a three-dimensional volume. Such volumes can then be used to diagnose a wide range of conditions and allow for volumetric measurements of organs. In this work, we tackle the problem of reconstructing CT images from biplanar x-rays only. X-rays are widely available and even if the CT reconstructed from these radiographs is not a replacement of a complete CT in the diagnostic setting, it might serve to spare the patients from radiation where a CT is only acquired for rough measurements such as determining organ size. We propose a novel method based on the transformer architecture, by framing the underlying task as a language translation problem. Radiographs and CT images are first embedded into latent quantized codebook vectors using two different autoencoder networks. We then train a GPT model, to reconstruct the codebook vectors of the CT image, conditioned on the codebook vectors of the x-rays and show that this approach leads to realistic looking images. To encourage further research in this direction, we make our code publicly available on GitHub: https://github.com/FirasGit/transformers_ct_reconstruction.

Keywords: Chest Radiography · Computed Tomography · Multi Modal · Transformers

1 Introduction

In clinical practice, two widely adopted imaging techniques are X-ray radiographs and computed tomography (CT) scans. They serve as essential diagnostic

J. M. Wolterink et al. (Eds.): SASHIMI 2023, LNCS 14288, pp. 1–10, 2023.
https://doi.org/10.1007/978-3-031-44689-4_1

tools for radiologists and are used to examine the human body as well as detect abnormalities or injuries [6, 11] While both employ X-rays to provide radiologists with an image of the patients body, radiographs are only capable of generating two-dimensional (2D) projections of the body, while CT scans allow for more detailed three-dimensional (3D) image. The latter is possible, as CT images are computationally constructed by composing multiple X-rays taken from different directions into a detailed cross-section image of the body. As a longer exposure time is required to construct such 3D volumes, CT scans are associated with a high radiation dose. However, in some cases, a detailed image is not necessary, and CT imaging is used solely to measure the size and extent of organs like the liver before surgery. Radiographs, on the other hand, cannot provide quantitative measurements in terms of volume, but they are more cost-effective and radiation-friendly than CT scans.

As both imaging modalities are based on X-rays, methods exist to transform the 3D CT scans into matching 2D radiographs. However, this transformation leads to a loss of information, as many details of the image will be removed. Thus, the opposite direction, i.e., transforming a 2D radiograph into a 3D CT scan is not easily possible. Nonetheless, enabling such reconstructions can provide significant benefits, as synthesizing a CT image from existing radiographs could help reduce the patient's exposure to radiation from a CT scan and assist surgeons in their planning process, allowing them to more accurately assess the patient's anatomy.

Over the years, several methods have been proposed that attempt to convert radiographs into corresponding CT scans [15–17, 19]. These methods are largely based on convolutional neural networks (CNNs) and employ GAN-based [8] discriminators to synthesize realistic looking images. However, such network designs typically require unsymmetric encoder-decoder networks, in which a separate encoder branch is needed for each 2D projection [19]. Moreover, GAN-based methods are known to suffer from mode collapse, resulting in similar looking images [1].

More recently, the transformer architecture [18] has been introduced and has shown a remarkable performance in text-to-image generation tasks [7, 14]. New images are thereby generated in an autoregressive manner by modelling the joint distribution over the input tokens. Contrary to previous methods that rely on CNNs, in this study we built upon the recent progress of the transformer architecture and frame the cross-modality transfer as a language translation problem and by doing so leverage the power of transformers to convert monoplanar and biplanar radiographs into corresponding CT scans.

2   Materials and Methods

2.1   Dataset

We train and test our model on the publicly available LIDC-IDRI dataset [2, 3, 5] (https://wiki.cancerimagingarchive.net/). This dataset consists of 1,018 diagnostic and lung-cancer screening thoracic CT scans from 1,010 patients. The data

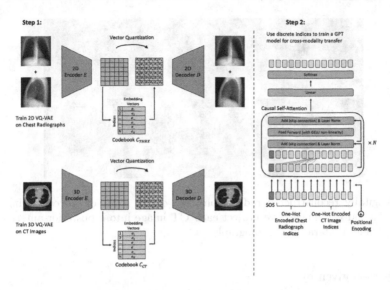

Fig. 1. Model architecture. In a first step, two different VQ-GAN models are trained: A 2D version which is used to transform the biplanar chest radiographs into a set of discrete codebook indices and a 3D version used to convert the CT image volumes into another set of codebook indices. By framing the underlying problem as a language translation problem, we then train a GPT model that, given the indices of the chest radiographs, autoregressively learns to generate indices corresponding to the CT volumes.

was collected from seven academic centers and eight medical imaging companies. In order to use this data to train our models, we apply a number of pre-processing steps: First, we convert the voxel values of each CT into Hounsfield units. Subsequently, we resample each volume into an isotropic voxel spacing of 1mm in all directions and center crop or pad each volume such that the resulting image is of shape $320 \times 320 \times 320$ (height, width, depth). In a final step, we resize the image into the shape $120 \times 120 \times 120$ and normalize each image to the range between -1 and 1. We proceed by splitting the pre-processed data into a training (70%, n=707 patients), validation (20%, n=202 patients) and testing split (20%, n=101 patients).

Digitally Reconstructed Radiographs The dataset mentioned above consists primarily of CT images without corresponding radiographs captured in lateral or posterior-anterior view. Consequently, we generated synthetic chest radiographs in both views (see Fig. 2) via digitally reconstructed radiographs [12]. More precisely, given a CT volume x and the voxel depth d_i (in direction of the projection) for each voxel i in the image, we first convert the voxel values from Hounsfield units to their corresponding linear attenuation coefficients u_i. The digitally reconstructed radiograph can then be constructed by computing

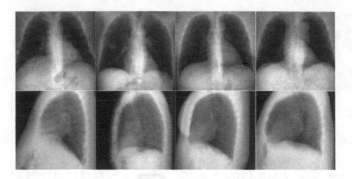

Fig. 2. Digitally reconstructed radiographs. To create a set of corresponding chest radiographs and CT images, we project each CT image into a posterior-anterior view radiograph and a lateral view radiograph.

the projection given by

$$x_{\text{projection}} = I_0 \exp(-\sum_{i=1}^{n} u_i d_i) \tag{1}$$

The factor I_0 thereby denotes the signal intensity of the X-ray photons that we arbitrarily set to 1keV and n denotes the number of voxels that the ray passes through.

2.2 Model

In contrast to previous work that mainly proposes the use of unsymmetric CNN-based encoder-decoder architectures with a discriminator loss for converting radiographs into CT scans, we make use of a transformer-based method (see Fig. 1). Fundamentally, we frame the underlying task as a language translation problem, in which a set of discrete tokens from language A (i.e., the radiographs) is translated into a set of discrete tokens from language B (i.e., the CT scans). In the following we will briefly introduce the concept of vector quantization with regard to the VQ-VAE [13] and the VQ-GAN [7] models. Subsequently, we show how the GPT [4] model can then be used to perform the modality transfer.

Vector Quantization. In order to treat the underlying problem as a language translation problem, where we go from a discrete set of tokens from language A to a discrete set of tokens from language B, we first have convert the two-dimensional chest radiographs and the three-dimensional CT volumes into such discrete representations. One popular approach for obtaining discrete representations with a reasonably sized alphabet (represented as a codebook in the following) is through the use of a VQ-VAE [13]. In essence, an encoder neural network E is used to compress the image into a latent dimension with a continuous feature space. This feature space is then quantized by mapping each feature vector onto its nearest neighbor in a learnable codebook C with N entries. The resulting quantized feature representation is fed into a decoder neural network D trained to reconstruct the image. The loss can therefore be expressed as

$$\mathcal{L}_{\mathcal{VQ}} = \|x - \hat{x}\|^2 + \|\text{sg}[E(x)] - e\|_2^2 + \|\text{sg}[e] - E(x)\|_2^2 \tag{2}$$

where x denotes the input, $\hat{x}$ denotes the reconstructed output, e represents the vector quantized feature vector and sg[.] indicates the stop-gradient operation. Following Esser et al.'s improvements in their proposed VQ-GAN model [7], we add a perceptual loss [10] $\mathcal{L}_P$ and a discriminator loss [9] $\mathcal{L}_G$ to the output of the decoder. The discriminator is thereby trained to distinguish between the real input image x and the reconstructed output image $\hat{x}$, which has been found to produce superior reconstructions. We extend the original 2D formulation of the model to also support 3D images by replacing the 2D convolution operations by 3D operations and modifying the perceptual loss term to be the mean perceptual loss over all depth slices in the 3D volume. Given both versions of the model, we train the 2D VQ-GAN to create a discrete representation of size $16 \times 16 \times 1$ (height, width, depth) for the lateral and posterior-anterior views of the radiographs (i.e., one network is trained for both views) with a codebook C_{THRX} of size $N = 8192$. Similarly, we train the 3D VQ-GAN (with a latent dimension of $16 \times 16 \times 16$) on the CT images using a codebook C_{CT} of the same size N.

GPT-Based Language Translation. To perform the task of translating token representations of the biplanar chest radiographs, which are specified by indices in the codebook C_{THRX}, into token representations associated with their corresponding CT image, which are specified by indices in the codebook C_{CT}, we train an autoregressive GPT model. More precisely, we first convert the set of indices that represent each image into a one-hot encoded representation (i.e., the codebook vector at position 3 would be encoded into the vector representation $(0, 0, 1, ...)^T$ of size N). Subsequently we order the resulting token representations by first listing all tokens pertaining to the radiograph in posterior-anterior view, followed by the tokens pertaining to the radiograph in lateral view and finally the token representations of the ground truth CT scan. Additionally, a start of sentence token (SOS) is prepended to the set of tokens, which is used to later prompt the GPT model with the token generation. A learnable positional encoding vector is then added to each token. These token representations are then sequentially passed through a series of transformer blocks, where the number of blocks l is set to 8 in our model. Within each transformer block, a causal self-attention mechanism is employed, thereby restricting each token from attending to tokens that come after it in the sequence, allowing it to only attend to tokens that precede it. The output of the last transformer block is subsequently passed through a linear layer as well as a softmax layer to arrive at the prediction, which represents the probability of the next token in the sequence. The cross-entropy loss is used as the loss function.

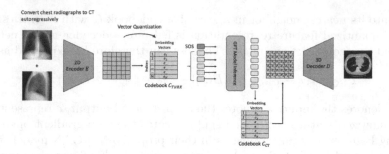

Fig. 3. Inference procedure. After the respective models have been trained we can convert a set of unseen chest radiographs to a synthetic CT volume by first converting the chest radiographs into their discrete latent representation. The codebook indices of this latent representation are then used to autoregressively infer new set of indices that correspond to the latent representation of the CT volume. In a final step, the new set of discrete indices is converted to the CT volume by feeding them into the decoder of the previously trained 3D VQ-GAN

Inference. After completing the training process for all networks, we can proceed to generate synthetic CT images. To achieve this, we first transform a set of unseen radiographs captured in posterior-anterior and lateral views into their discrete token representations using the previously trained 2D VQ-GAN. These representations are then concatenated, such that the tokens originating from the posterior-anterior view are listed first, followed by the tokens from the lateral view. Subsequently, we feed this concatenated representation into the trained GPT model to prompt the generation of tokens that correspond to the CT images in an autoregressive manner. The generation process continues until a total of J tokens are generated, where J denotes the number of indices required to represent the latent representation of the CT image. In a final step, we utilize the previously trained decoder of the 3D VQ GAN to convert the latent representation of the CT image into an actual synthetic CT image (see Fig. 3). It is worth noting that this method also enables the creation of synthetic CT images when using solely a single radiograph as input (i.e., the radiograph captured in posterior-anterior view). This is achieved by feeding the single radiograph to the GPT model and prompting it to generate tokens that correspond to the radiograph captured in the lateral view and the CT image.

2.3   Training Settings

All our models were trained on an NVIDIA RTX A6000 and were implemented using PyTorch v2.1.0. The VQ-GAN models were trained for 500 epochs and we chose the models that performed best (i.e., resulted in the lowest loss) on the validation set to encode and decode the images. The GPT model was trained for a total of 300 epochs, and similarly, the model that demonstrated the best performance in terms of the lowest loss on the validation set was selected for evaluation.

3   Results

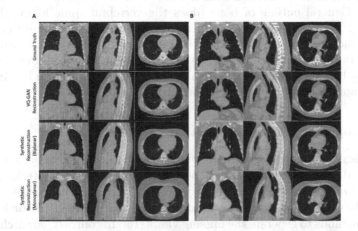

Fig. 4. Synthetic CT images produced by our model using radiographs from the test dataset. (A) and (B) denote two different samples. The top row shows the ground truth CT images, while the second row shows reconstructed CT images using the trained 3D VQ GAN model. The third row displays synthetic CT images generated by our model when presented with radiographs taken in posterior-anterior and lateral views, and the fourth row displays synthetic CT images generated by the model when only provided with a single radiograph in posterior-anterior view.

3.1   Biplanar CT Reconstruction

For biplanar reconstruction, i.e. the reconstruction of the full CT volume from both a posterior-anterior and a lateral radiograph, we found that the generated volume looked realistic as a whole (see Fig. 4), but that fine details of the organs such as lung structure or the internal structure of the heart or the bones were not reconstructed faithfully. This limitation primarily stemmed from the reconstruction quality of the VQ-GAN model, as its decoder is used to construct the CT images based on the generated tokens. While the model accurately represented the shape of internal structures, which was its main objective, its performance was diminished when evaluated quantitatively due to the lack of fine details. To address this, we chose to assess the performance of our approach by utilizing a human expert, as their evaluations of the depicted structures are more reliable.

A radiologist with 10 years of experience compared the GPT-reconstructed CT volumes using radiographs from the test dataset with the original volumes and rated the following categories on a scale from 0 (= no agreement between original and reconstructed structure) to 5 (= perfect agreement between original and reconstructed structure): Inner structure of the heart (distribution of heart chambers and vessels): 1.8 ± 1.2. Form of the heart (outline of the heart shape):

4.2 ± 0.7. Inner structure of the lungs (distribution of vessels and bronchi): 1.7 ± 1.5. Form of the lungs (outline of the lungs): 4.3 ± 0.6. Inner structure of bones (can structure be inferred from the bones, such as osteoporotic changes?): 0.7 ± 0.3. General outline of bone (does the vertebral spine follow the same pattern, e.g. skoliosis, kyphosis): 4.1 ± 0.7. These categories were chosen to both rate fine details (inner structure) and the more general anatomical outline of larger structures. The results were in line with expectations as organ outlines can already be seen on radiographs, while the inner structures are barely visible on radiographs due to the superposition effect.

3.2   Monoplanar CT Reconstruction

In the clinical setting, radiographs are not routinely performed in both posterior-anterior and lateral acquisition schemes, but often only in posterior-anterior position. Previous methods either involve modifying the encoder branches to accommodate the varying number of input images or utilize PCA or k-nearest neighbor methods to generate the missing views [15]. In contrast, our architecture is flexible in the sense that it can accomodate for missing data and reconstruct full CT volumes from posterior-anterior radiographs alone without any changes to the model. Therefore, we generated CT examinations from these radiographs only and repeated the experiments with the radiologist. The ratings were slightly decreased, but showed the same trend: Inner structure of the heart: 1.7 ± 1.1. Form of the heart: 3.9 ± 0.8. Inner structure of the lungs: 1.7 ± 1.6. Form of the lungs: 3.9 ± 0.7. Inner structure of bones: 0.7 ± 0.4. General outline of bone: 4.1 ± 0.6. Again, this was in line with our expectations: As before, it can be seen that organ outlines are easier to reconstruct than fine details and it can also be expected that the reconstruction is less faithful as compared to the situation where an additional lateral radiograph serves as an additional source of information.

4   Conclusion

In this work, we developed and presented a novel transformer-based method capable of converting a set of 2D radiographs into a corresponding 3D CT scan. We demonstrate that this model can generate CT scans that largely capture the outline and form of the heart, lungs and bones accurately. This information can potentially be used clinically to measure the size of organs, as for such purposes only the general outline is necessary. We also found that fine details, such as the parenchymal structure of the lung, or the internal structure of the heart can not reliably be reconstructed. This is understandable since this information is most likely not sufficiently presented by two projections alone. Importantly, this is a limitation that is shared by all methods of creating 3D volumes from 2D radiographs, but that is often overlooked and not sufficiently evaluated. Furthermore, we show that the transformer-based method allows for a reconstruction of CT images based on single posterio-anterior radiographs, without the need of explicitly modifying any parts of the architecture. In addition, incorporating information of other modalities, such as laboratory values which are obtained next to the radiographs, can easily be performed by inputting these elements as tokens into the GPT model. This could be useful in cases where these laboratory values are informative of structural changes (e.g., brain natriuretic peptide as an indicator for enlargement of certain heart chambers). In future work we will assess the performance of our model on large-scale CT image databases to fully leverage the power of scalable transformer architectures. Moreover, exploring further directions that improve the latent space representation in the VQ-GAN bottleneck, such as increased codebook size or compression rate, may be worthwhile.

Acknowledgement. The authors acknowledge the National Cancer Institute and the Foundation for the National Institutes of Health, and their critical role in the creation of the free publicly available LIDC/IDRI Database used in this study.

References

1. Arjovsky, M., Chintala, S., Bottou, L.: Wasserstein GAN (Dec 2017). arXiv: 1701.07875 [cs, stat]
2. Armato, S.G., et al.: The lung image database consortium (LIDC) and image database resource initiative (IDRI): a completed reference database of lung nodules on CT scans. Med. Phys. **38**(2), 915–931 (2011). https://www.ncbi.nlm.nih.gov/pmc/articles/PMC3041807/
3. Armato III, S.G.: Data From LIDC-IDRI (2015). https://wiki.cancerimaging archive.net/x/rgAe, version Number: 4 Type: dataset
4. Brown, T.B., et al.: Language Models are Few-Shot Learners (Jul 2020) arXiv:2005.14165
5. Clark, K., et al.: The cancer imaging archive (TCIA): maintaining and operating a public information repository. J. Digital Imaging **26**(6), 1045–1057 (2013), https://www.ncbi.nlm.nih.gov/pmc/articles/PMC3824915/
6. Dey, R., Lu, Z., Hong, Y.: Diagnostic classification of lung nodules using 3D neural networks. In: 2018 IEEE 15th International Symposium on Biomedical Imaging (ISBI 2018), pp. 774–778 (Apr 2018). ISSN: 1945–8452
7. Esser, P., Rombach, R., Ommer, B.: Taming transformers for high-resolution image synthesis. In: Proceedings of the IEEE/CVF Conference on Computer Vision and Pattern Recognition, pp. 12873–12883 (2021). https://openaccess.thecvf.com/content/CVPR2021/html/Esser_Taming_Transformers_for_High-Resolution_Imag e_Synthesis_CVPR_2021_paper.html
8. Goodfellow, I., et al.: Generative Adversarial Nets. In: Advances in Neural Information Processing Systems, vol. 27. Curran Associates, Inc. (2014)
9. Isola, P., Zhu, J.Y., Zhou, T., Efros, A.A.: Image-to-image translation with conditional adversarial networks. In: 2017 IEEE Conference on Computer Vision and Pattern Recognition (CVPR), pp. 5967–5976 (Jul 2017). https://doi.org/10.1109/CVPR.2017.632, ISSN: 1063-6919
10. Johnson, J., Alahi, A., Fei-Fei, L.: Perceptual losses for real-time style transfer and super-resolution. In: Leibe, B., Matas, J., Sebe, N., Welling, M. (eds.) ECCV 2016. LNCS, vol. 9906, pp. 694–711. Springer, Cham (2016). https://doi.org/10.1007/978-3-319-46475-6_43

11. Khader, F., et al.: Artificial intelligence for clinical interpretation of bedside chest radiographs. Radiology, 220510 (2022). https://pubs.rsna.org/doi/10.1148/radiol. 220510
12. Milickovic, N., Baltast, D., Giannouli, S., Lahanas, M., Zamboglou, N.: CT imaging based digitally reconstructed radiographs and their application in brachytherapy. Phys. Med. Biol. **45**(10), 2787–2800 (2000)
13. van den Oord, A., Vinyals, O., kavukcuoglu, K.: Neural discrete representation learning. In: Advances in Neural Information Processing Systems, vol. 30, pp. 6309–6318. Curran Associates, Inc. (2017)
14. Ramesh, A., et al.: Zero-Shot Text-to-Image Generation (Feb 2021). arXiv:2102.12092
15. Schock, J., et al.: Monoplanar CT reconstruction with GANs. In: 2022 Eleventh International Conference on Image Processing Theory, Tools and Applications (IPTA), pp. 1–6 (Apr 2022), ISSN: 2154–512X
16. Shen, L., Zhao, W., Xing, L.: Patient-specific reconstruction of volumetric computed tomography images from a single projection view via deep learning. Nat. Biomed. Eng. **3**(11), 880–888 (2019). www.nature.com/articles/s41551-019-0466-4
17. Shiode, R., et al.: 2D–3D reconstruction of distal forearm bone from actual X-ray images of the wrist using convolutional neural networks. Scientific Reports 11(1), 15249 (2021). www.nature.com/articles/s41598-021-94634-2
18. Vaswani, A., et al.: Attention is all you need. In: Advances in Neural Information Processing Systems, vol. 30. Curran Associates, Inc. (2017). www.proceedings. neurips.cc/paper/2017/hash/3f5ee243547dee91fbd053c1c4a845aa-Abstract.html
19. Ying, X., Guo, H., Ma, K., Wu, J., Weng, Z., Zheng, Y.: X2CT-GAN: reconstructing CT from biplanar X-Rays with generative adversarial networks (May 2019). arXiv:1905.06902

Super-Resolution Segmentation Network for Inner-Ear Tissue Segmentation

Ziteng Liu[1]([✉]), Yubo Fan[1], Ange Lou[1], and Jack H. Noble[1,2]

[1] Department of Computer Science, Vanderbilt University, Nashville, USA
ziteng.liu@vanderbilt.edu
[2] Department of Electrical and Computer Engineering, Vanderbilt University,
Nashville, USA

Abstract. Cochlear implants (CIs) are considered the standard-of-care treatment for profound sensory-based hearing loss. Several groups have proposed computational models of the cochlea in order to study the neural activation patterns in response to CI stimulation. However, most of the current implementations either rely on high-resolution histological images that cannot be customized for CI users or CT images that lack the spatial resolution to show cochlear structures. In this work, we propose to use a deep learning-based method to obtain CT level tissue labels using patient CT images. Experiments showed that the proposed super-resolution segmentation architecture achieved very good performance on the inner-ear tissue segmentation. Our best-performing model (0.871) outperformed the UNet (0.746), VNet (0.853), nnUNet (0.861), TransUNet (0.848), and SRGAN (0.780) in terms of mean dice score.

Keywords: Cochlear implant · super-resolution · segmentation

1 Introduction

Cochlear implants (CIs) are considered the standard-of-care treatment for profound sensory-based hearing loss. With over 700,000 recipients worldwide [15], CI is undoubtedly one of the most successful neural prostheses in history. Several groups have proposed computational models of the cochlea in order to simulate the neural activation patterns in response to CI stimulation, which can provide objective information for CI programming. Noble et al. proposed image-guided CI programming (IGCIP) techniques where CT-based intra-cochlear segmentation is used to estimate the electro-neural interface [18]. Although experiments have shown that IGCIP significantly improves hearing outcomes in clinical settings [16,17], it estimates the neural response in a relatively coarse manner where only the spatial relationship between CI electrodes and neural sites is used. Frijns et al. proposed a rotationally symmetric model of cochlea [6] and Kalkman et al. proposed an electro-anatomical model (EAM) where a tissue label map of the inner ear is generated [11], they used boundary element method to solve for the voltage distribution in the electrically stimulated cochlea. Whiten *et al.* also

J. M. Wolterink et al. (Eds.): SASHIMI 2023, LNCS 14288, pp. 11–20, 2023.
https://doi.org/10.1007/978-3-031-44689-4_2

created an EAM model of human cochlea, while they used the finite difference method to solve for the electric potential distribution [24]. Although these methods are useful to explore the mechanics of CI and neural response, they rely on 3D tissue electrical resistivity maps built based on histological images and cannot be applied in-vivo or customized for CI implant users. Malherbe et al. used patient specific EAMs based on CT images [14]. However, their method relies on manual point selection in CT images that don't have fine enough resolution to show intra-cochlear structures. To overcome this, Cakir et al. developed an approach to create a high resolution patient-specific class map using multi-atlas segmentation, where CTs with manual tissue class labels are non-rigidly registered to the patient CT [2]. The registration is done with a thin plate spline transformation that uses points in an active-shape-model based segmentation of the scalae structures as landmarks. As these landmarks are on the cochlear surface, the classification of tissues distant from the cochlea tends to not be very accurate, however, accurate labels are critical for creating an accurate EAM.

Thanks to the rapid development of deep learning, convolutional neural networks (CNN) have been widely applied for medical image segmentation tasks and achieved state-of-the-art performance with leading network architectures [8]. Several deep-learning-based cochlear anatomy segmentation methods have been proposed using CT images [5,23,26], but they mainly focus on the intra-cochlear anatomy. Deep learning methods for medical images super-resolution are also widely discussed [13]. A number of novel methods were proposed to synthesize higher-resolution medical images of the same modality [20,21,25]. However, a post-processing step is still needed for further classification, diagnosis, or segmentation when using these methods.

Herein, we propose the super-resolution segmentation network (SRSegN) for CTs of the inner ear. Briefly, we inherit the encoder-decoder architecture of UNet [22] and add an up-sampling branch that extracts features from the low-resolution images of input and up-samples the feature maps progressively. The pyramid feature maps from the encoder and the up-sampling branch will be concatenated to corresponding features in the decoder. As an end-to-end architecture, SRSegN can generate a segmentation that has 8 times higher resolution than the input CT image. Experiments showed that the proposed architecture can produce high-quality high-resolution segmentation.

2   Related Works

Semantic Segmentation. Semantic segmentation identifies the class label of each pixel in the image. One of the most widely used and most well-known architectures for medical image segmentation is the U-Net [22]. By introducing the skip connection between the layers of equal resolution in the encoder and decoder, good localization and the use of context are possible at the same time. The success of U-Net has attracted a lot of attention in the area of image segmentation and a number of variants such as Attention U-Net [19] and VNet [1] were proposed to further improve the performance of U-Net. One of the most successful variants is nnU-Net, which features the automatic configuration of U-Net models. The nnU-Net was tested on 23 public datasets of biomedical images and outperforms most existing approaches in 2020 [10]. Another novel U-Net variant is the TransUNet [3]. By introducing the visual transformer (ViT) [4] in the encoder, TransUNet stated to have better performance. Due to the efficiency of multi-head self-attention (MSA) in encoding spatial information globally, transformer-based models recently dominate the field of semantic segmentation. Despite the impressive performance of visual transformer, MSA focuses only on spatial attention and has limited localization ability. To address this problem, Guo et al. proposed a convolution-based attention mechanism named multi-scale convolutional attention network (MSCAN) [7].

Image Super-resolution. Super-resolution (SR) refers to the process of increasing the spatial resolution of images. Medical images in real life suffer from low spatial resolution due to limited irradiation dose, relatively short acquisition time, or hardware limits. In the current work our goal is not SR, but rather high resolution tissue type segmentation. However, many relevant deep-learning-based SR methods have been widely explored, and more recently, more methods have been proposed for medical images. One of the key problems for image SR is how to perform upsampling. Based on the location of upsampling layers, most SR models can be classified into three frameworks: pre-upsampling model, post-upsampling model, and progressive upsampling model. Ledig et al. proposed the SRGAN [12] for single image SR problem based on the generative adversarial network (GAN) and achieved state-of-the-art results. In the area of medical imaging, different methods have been proposed to synthesize SR images [20,21,25]. SynthSR [9] proposed a very straightforward approach where they upsample low-resolution MRI with a trilinear interpolation and then synthesize the SR images with a 3D UNet, and showed impressive performance (Fig. 1).

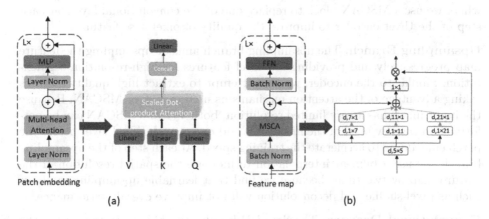

Fig. 1. Two attention mechanisms we tested in our models. (a) Visual transformer (ViT). (b) Multi-scale convolutional attention network (MSCAN) blocks.

3   Method

Given that patient specific EAMs need CT level resolution (0.036mm) tissue class maps to simulate the electro-neural interface, and the resolution of pre-operative patient CTs is usually between 0.2 to 0.3mm, our goal is to predict a tissue class map that is 8 times higher resolution than the input CT image. Unlike the previous strategies, we proposed an end-to-end architecture, in which a low-resolution image is upsampled progressively in the neural network and the high-resolution segmentation is obtained directly. With low-resolution input, the proposed method naturally has a bigger receptive field than architectures that use interpolated images. In this section, we introduce the proposed architecture in detail.

Encoder. Like most encoder-decoder architectures, the encoder downsamples feature maps with pooling layers. Each pooling operator downsamples the feature maps by a factor of two, and then convolutional layers increase the number of channels by a factor of two. The receptive field grows and higher-level features are revealed as the size of feature maps decreases. In order to explore the effect of the attention mechanism, we implemented three types of encoders: the fully convolutional encoder, the ViT-convolution encoder, and the MSCAN encoder. As shown in Fig. 2, the fully convolutional encoder consists of two convolutional layers followed by a pooling layer at each step. Figure 3(c) shows the architecture of a ViT-based encoder variant where we use convolutional and pooling layers to extract and downsample features from the input image before sending the features to a ViT where the patch embeddings are learned for every flattened 2D patch of the feature map. The hidden features from the ViT are reshaped to reconstruct the feature map and since we use a patch size of 11, the reconstructed feature map is of the same size as the input of the ViT. As for the MSCAN encoder (shown in Fig. 3(d)), it follows the architecture proposed in SegNeXt, where we use a MSCAN block to replace one of the convolutional layers at each step of the UNet encoder to improve the quality of pixel-wise features.

Upsampling Branch. The upsampling branch aims at upsampling the feature map progressively and providing low level features for high-resolution segmentation. Similar to the encoder, we also attempt to extract high-quality features taking advantage of the attention mechanisms used in ViT or MSCAN. Because the input image has a very limited resolution, both ViT and MSCAN can be performed on the raw pixel of the image. We add one convolutional layer before the patch embedding to accelerate the training speed. At each step of the upsampling branch, we use a bilinear interpolation to increase the spatial resolution of the feature map by two times because we find that learnable upsampling methods such as pixel-shuffle and deconvolution will not improve overall performance.

Convolutional Decoder. The decoder decodes the hidden features from the encoder by upsampling the features in multiple steps and outputs the final segmentation masks with a segmentation head. Given the number of downsampling operators in the encoder m and the number of upsampling operators in the upsampling branch n, the total number of upsampling steps of the decoder is m+n. Features from the encoder and the upsampling branch will be concatenated to corresponding features in the decoder that have the same size.

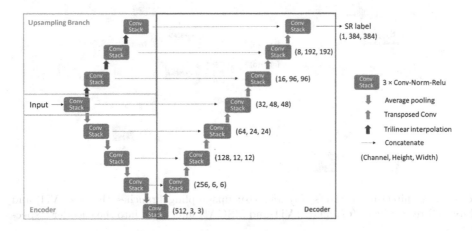

Fig. 2. Overview of the proposed architecture.

4 Experiments

4.1 Dataset

We constructed our dataset using 6 specimens. Each of them has a pair of CT scans (0.3 mm isotropic) and CT scans (0.0375mm isotropic) that have been rigidly registered with each other. Then a high-resolution manual label was obtained using the CT. Our label maps contain four classes: air, soft tissue (including neural tissue, electrolytic fluid, and soft tissue), bone, and the background. We clipped the values in raw CT images to remove potential artifacts, and then normalization was performed for every image. In the experiments described below, we used leave-one-out cross-validation, where the data from one specimen was chosen as the testing set and the others were randomly split into training set and validation set according to a ratio of 4:1. When a 2D network was trained, the training set contained 9476 2D slices from all three directions of the processed volumes. For SRGAN and our proposed architectures, low-resolution CT slices were cropped to 48×48 so the output label map size was 384×384. For other architectures, upsampled CT slices or volumes that have the same resolution with our high-resolution labels were used as input. We applied random cropping, random rotation, random flipping and random scaling (0.75 to 1.25) as data augmentation methods with a probability of 0.5. During inference, images were predicted using a sliding window that overlaps by half the size of a patch for adjacent predictions. For 2D networks, CTs were linearly interpolated

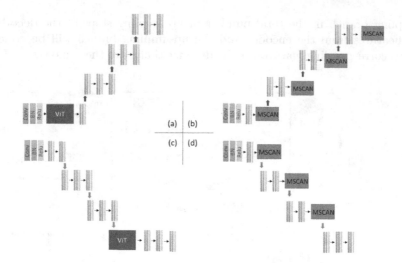

Fig. 3. Architecture Variants: (a) and (b): upsampling branches that use ViT and MSCAN respectively. (c) and (d): ViT and MSCAN integrated into the encoder respectively.

in the axial direction and then the resulting volumes were inferenced in a slice-by-slice fashion. The predicted 2D slices are stacked together to reconstruct the 3D prediction for evaluation.

4.2   Implementation Details

All the architectures we tested are implemented in PyTorch and trained on a single NVIDIA A5000 GPU. Our proposed architecture was trained with SGD with momentum 0.9. We used the learning rate warm-up for the first 2000 iterations followed by a cosine learning rate decay scheduler with max epoch = 1000. All models were trained with cross-entropy loss and dice coefficient loss that ignore the background. All models were trained with a batch size of 2 and a global random seed of 42 was used for the Pytorch and Numpy random generators. To perform fair comparison between architectures, we removed the post-processing steps in the nnUNet pipeline. As for the ViT we used in SRSegN, the hidden size, number of layers, MLP size, and number of heads were set to 768, 8, 3072, and 12, respectively. We use an MLP ratio of 4 and a depth of 6 when MSCAN is used in our architecture. The average training time for SRSegViT is 42.7 h.

4.3   Model Variants

We attempted to find the best combination out of our different implementations of the upsampling branch and the encoder, but we did not try to use the attention mechanisms in both substructures at the same time because that would be too computationally expensive. To perform an ablation study, we also show the result without the upsampling branch. The ViT we used consists of 12 transformer layers of 16-head self-attention. We adopted the pre-trained ViT on large datasets by Dosovitskiy et al. [4] and fine-tuned the transformer on our dataset. The pre-trained prediction head of the original ViT was removed and the positional embedding was interpolated to match the number of patches in our architecture. As for MSCAN, we trained those blocks from scratch.

Table 1. Dice coefficient scores of the segmentation results

	Architecture	DSC-Air	DSC-Tissue	DSC-Bone	DSC-Avg
Post	UNet (2D)	0.652 ± 0.033	0.693 ± 0.015	0.719 ± 0.014	0.688 ± 0.019
	UNet (3D)	0.534 ± 0.026	0.697 ± 0.016	0.741 ± 0.008	0.657 ± 0.020
Pre-up.	UNet (2D)	0.782 ± 0.021	0.629 ± 0.023	0.828 ± 0.017	0.746 ± 0.025
	VNet	0.883 ± 0.011	0.758 ± 0.013	0.918 ± 0.016	0.853 ± 0.009
	nnUNet (3D)	0.892 ± 0.038	0.769 ± 0.010	0.921 ± 0.018	0.861 ± 0.015
	TransUNet	0.867 ± 0.031	0.746 ± 0.009	0.931 ± 0.012	0.848 ± 0.016
Progressive up.	SRGAN	0.835 ± 0.014	0.652 ± 0.048	0.855 ± 0.026	0.780 ± 0.021
	ours Up. branch Encoder	DSC-Air	DSC-Tissue	DSC-Bone	DSC-Avg.
	None CNN	0.782 ± 0.014	0.628 ± 0.039	0.829 ± 0.012	0.746 ± 0.027
	CNN CNN	0.892 ± 0.009	0.740 ± 0.019	0.935 ± 0.017	0.855 ± 0.020
	ViT CNN	$\mathbf{0.905 \pm 0.025}$	$\mathbf{0.772 \pm 0.017}$	$\mathbf{0.935 \pm 0.011}$	$\mathbf{0.871 \pm 0.013}$
	MSCAN CNN	0.862 ± 0.024	0.756 ± 0.022	0.925 ± 0.036	0.847 ± 0.023
	CNN MSCAN	0.893 ± 0.010	0.750 ± 0.029	0.927 ± 0.019	0.856 ± 0.014

Table 2. The number of parameters in each architecture

Architecture	UNet 2D	VNet	nnUNet 3D	TransUNet	SRGAN	SRSegN-ViT
Num. of parameters	22.0 M	45.6M	65.9 M	105.6 M	1.4 M	79.3 M

4.4 Results

We compared the segmentation results of the proposed methods with UNet, nnUNet, TransUNet and SRGAN. Table 1 shows the performance of different architectures evaluated on our dataset. We show the mean dice coefficient scores $\pm$ standard deviation and the highest scores in each column are presented in bold. The "Post-up.", "Pre-up.", and "Progressive up." refers to the three different segmentation pipelines. The post-upsampling pipline uses trilinear interpolation to up-sample low resolution segmentation results and the pre-upsampling architectures require a pre-processing step where we upsampled the low-resolution CT $\times 8$ using trilinear interpolation. Experiments show that the proposed architecture has the best performance when ViT is integrated into the upsampling

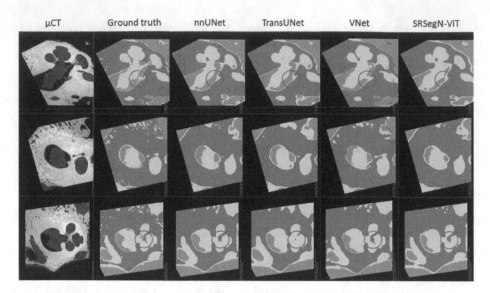

Fig. 4. Ground truth and segmentation results using different architectures. In label maps: Yellow - soft tissue. Green - Air. Red - Bone. (Color figure online)

branch (as shown in Fig. 2(c)), we refer to it as SRSegViT. SRSegViT is significantly better (two-sample paired t-tests, $p<0.02$ with nnUNet and $p<0.01$ with others) than other tested architectures. Figure 4 shows a qualitative comparison of the segmentation outcomes of different architectures. The red circles in the figure represent locations where the segmentation of our proposed method is qualitatively better than other segmentation as the segmentation of SRSegViT has more high-frequency details. Table 2 shows the number of parameters of each model.

5   Discussion and Conclusions

In this paper, we introduced an architecture for SR image segmentation of the inner-ear tissue. Unlike other SR architectures that relies on posterior segmentation methods to produce SR label maps, we provide an end-to-end method and achieved better performance than multiple state-of-the-art segmentation baselines. ViT-based encoder proved to be useful even on a limited dataset like ours by fine-tuning pre-trained transformers. The proposed methods, especially SRSegViT, achieves very good performance on the inner-ear tissue segmentation and such model could be critical for constructing accurate computational models for CI patients. In addition to the experiments shown in Table 1, we also explored the effects of different upsampling methods and loss functions. We found that: (1) learning-based upsampling methods do not affect the network performance significantly compared to interpolation. (2) Adversarial loss or perceptual loss is not helpful for the SR segmentation task, although a number of single-image SR methods benefited from them.

By removing or replacing the encoder with different architectures, we also showed the potential of the proposed architecture combining with other novel attention mechanisms. We are confident that this end-to-end architecture can be applied to many other medical or non-medical SR segmentation tasks. Our future work includes testing our model in clinical settings for CI patients and comparing the resulting electro-anatomical models with the ones generated by our traditional atlas-based method.

References

1. Abdollahi, A., Pradhan, B., Alamri, A.: Vnet: An end-to-end fully convolutional neural network for road extraction from high-resolution remote sensing data. IEEE Access **8**, 179424–179436 (2020)
2. Cakir, A., Dawant, B.M., Noble, J.H.: Development of a μCT-based patient-specific model of the electrically stimulated cochlea. In: Descoteaux, M., Maier-Hein, L., Franz, A., Jannin, P., Collins, D.L., Duchesne, S. (eds.) MICCAI 2017. LNCS, vol. 10433, pp. 773–780. Springer, Cham (2017). https://doi.org/10.1007/978-3-319-66182-7_88
3. Chen, J., et al.: Transunet: transformers make strong encoders for medical image segmentation. arXiv preprint arXiv:2102.04306 (2021)
4. Dosovitskiy, A., et al.: An image is worth 16x16 words: transformers for image recognition at scale. arXiv preprint arXiv:2010.11929 (2020)
5. Fan, Y., Zhang, D., Wang, J., Noble, J.H., Dawant, B.M.: Combining model-and deep-learning-based methods for the accurate and robust segmentation of the intra-cochlear anatomy in clinical head ct images. In: Medical Imaging 2020: Image Processing, vol. 11313, pp. 315–322. SPIE (2020)
6. Frijns, J.H., Briaire, J.J., Grote, J.J.: The importance of human cochlear anatomy for the results of modiolus-hugging multichannel cochlear implants. Otology Neu-rotol. **22**(3), 340–349 (2001)
7. Guo, M.H., Lu, C.Z., Hou, Q., Liu, Z., Cheng, M.M., Hu, S.M.: Segnext: rethinking convolutional attention design for semantic segmentation. arXiv preprint arXiv:2209.08575 (2022)
8. Hesamian, M.H., Jia, W., He, X., Kennedy, P.: Deep learning techniques for medical image segmentation: achievements and challenges. J. Digit. Imaging **32**(4), 582–596 (2019)
9. Iglesias, J.E., et al.: Joint super-resolution and synthesis of 1 mm isotropic mp-rage volumes from clinical MRI exams with scans of different orientation, resolution and contrast. Neuroimage **237**, 118206 (2021)
10. Isensee, F., Jaeger, P.F., Kohl, S.A., Petersen, J., Maier-Hein, K.H.: nnu-net: a self-configuring method for deep learning-based biomedical image segmentation. Nat. Methods **18**(2), 203–211 (2021)
11. Kalkman, R.K., Briaire, J.J., Frijns, J.H.: Current focussing in cochlear implants: an analysis of neural recruitment in a computational model. Hear. Res. **322**, 89–98 (2015)
12. Ledig, C., et al.: Photo-realistic single image super-resolution using a generative adversarial network. In: Proceedings of the IEEE Conference on Computer Vision and Pattern Recognition, pp. 4681–4690 (2017)

13. Li, Y., Sixou, B., Peyrin, F.: A review of the deep learning methods for medical images super resolution problems. Irbm **42**(2), 120–133 (2021)
14. Malherbe, T., Hanekom, T., Hanekom, J.: Constructing a three-dimensional electrical model of a living cochlear implant user's cochlea. Inter. J. Numerical Methods Biomed. Eng. **32**(7), e02751 (2016)
15. NIDCD: Nidcd nidcd fact sheet, hearing and balance: cochlear implants (2019). www.nidcd.nih.gov/health/cochlear-implants, (Accessed 10 Jan 2023)
16. Noble, J.H., Gifford, R.H., Hedley-Williams, A.J., Dawant, B.M., Labadie, R.F.: Clinical evaluation of an image-guided cochlear implant programming strategy. Audiol. Neurotol. **19**(6), 400–411 (2014)
17. Noble, J.H., et al.: Initial results with image-guided cochlear implant programming in children. Otology Neurotol. Official Publicat. Am. Otolog. Soc. Am. Neurotol. Soc. Euro. Acad. Otology Neurotol. **37**(2), e63 (2016)
18. Noble, J.H., Labadie, R.F., Gifford, R.H., Dawant, B.M.: Image-guidance enables new methods for customizing cochlear implant stimulation strategies. IEEE Trans. Neural Syst. Rehabil. Eng. **21**(5), 820–829 (2013)
19. Oktay, O., et al.: Attention u-net: learning where to look for the pancreas. arXiv preprint arXiv:1804.03999 (2018)
20. Park, J., Hwang, D., Kim, K.Y., Kang, S.K., Kim, Y.K., Lee, J.S.: Computed tomography super-resolution using deep convolutional neural network. Phys. Med. Biol. **63**(14), 145011 (2018)
21. Qiu, D., Cheng, Y., Wang, X., Zhang, X.: Multi-window back-projection residual networks for reconstructing covid-19 ct super-resolution images. Comput. Methods Programs Biomed. **200**, 105934 (2021)
22. Ronneberger, O., Fischer, P., Brox, T.: U-Net: convolutional networks for biomedical image segmentation. In: Navab, N., Hornegger, J., Wells, W.M., Frangi, A.F. (eds.) MICCAI 2015. LNCS, vol. 9351, pp. 234–241. Springer, Cham (2015). https://doi.org/10.1007/978-3-319-24574-4_28
23. Wang, J., Zhao, Y., Noble, J.H., Dawant, B.M.: Conditional generative adversarial networks for metal artifact reduction in CT images of the ear. In: Frangi, A.F., Schnabel, J.A., Davatzikos, C., Alberola-López, C., Fichtinger, G. (eds.) MICCAI 2018. LNCS, vol. 11070, pp. 3–11. Springer, Cham (2018). https://doi.org/10.1007/978-3-030-00928-1_1
24. Whiten, D.M.: Electro-anatomical models of the cochlear implant. Ph.D. thesis, Massachusetts Institute of Technology (2007)
25. You, C., et al.: Ct super-resolution gan constrained by the identical, residual, and cycle learning ensemble (gan-circle). IEEE Trans. Med. Imaging **39**(1), 188–203 (2019)
26. Zhang, D., Banalagay, R., Wang, J., Zhao, Y., Noble, J.H., Dawant, B.M.: Two-level training of a 3d u-net for accurate segmentation of the intra-cochlear anatomy in head cts with limited ground truth training data. In: Medical Imaging 2019: Image Processing, vol. 10949, pp. 45–52. SPIE (2019)

Multi-phase Liver-Specific DCE-MRI Translation via A Registration-Guided GAN

Jiyao Liu[1], Yuxin Li[2], Nannan Shi[3], Yuncheng Zhou[2], Shangqi Gao[2], Yuxin Shi[3], Xiao-Yong Zhang[1], and Xiahai Zhuang[2(✉)]

[1] Institute of Science and Technology for Brain-Inspired Intelligence, Fudan University, Shanghai, China
[2] School of Data Science, Fudan University, Shanghai, China
zhuangdata@aliyun.com
[3] Department of Radiology, Shanghai Public Health Clinical Center, Fudan University, Shanghai, China
https://zmiclab.github.io/projects.html

Abstract. In the diagnosis of liver lesions, Gd-EOB-DTPA-enhanced magnetic resonance imaging (MRI) at the hepatobiliary phase (GED-HBP) is particularly valuable. However, the acquisition of GED-HBP is more costly than that of a conventional dynamic contrast-enhanced MRI (DCE-MRI). This paper introduces a new dataset and a novel application of image translation from multi-phase DCE-MRIs into a virtual GED-HBP image (v-HBP) that could be used as a substitute for GED-HBP in clinical liver diagnosis. This is achieved by a generative adversarial network (GAN) with an auxiliary registration network, referred to as MrGAN. MrGAN bypasses the challenges from intra-sequence misalignments as well as inter-sequence misalignments. Additionally, MrGAN incorporates a pre-trained shape consistency network to promote local generation in the liver region. Extensive experiments demonstrated the superiority of our MrGAN over other state-of-the-art methods in terms of quantitative, qualitative, and clinical evaluations. We outlook the utility of our new dataset will extend to other problems beyond lesion detection due to the improved quality of the generated image. Code can be found at https://github.com/Jy-stdio/MrGAN.git.

Keywords: Liver DCE-MRI · Image translation · Image registration

1 Introduction

Gadolinium ethoxybenzyl diethy-lenetriaminepentaacetic acid (Gd-EOB-DTPA) is a liver-specific contrast enhancement agent presently used for the diagnosis of liver lesions in MRI [15]. As shown in Fig. 1, in contrast to the conventional contrast agent Gadopentetic acid (Gd-DTPA), Gd-EOB-DTPA enhances MRI

Contributed equally.

© The Author(s), under exclusive license to Springer Nature Switzerland AG 2023
J. M. Wolterink et al. (Eds.): SASHIMI 2023, LNCS 14288, pp. 21–31, 2023.
https://doi.org/10.1007/978-3-031-44689-4_3

at the hepatobiliary phase with higher sensitivity and accuracy in the detection of small hepatocellular carcinoma (HCC) [13]. However, acquiring GED-HBP is costly, attributed to the long acquisition time and expensive contrast agents [9]. Therefore, developing substitues using virtual images of GED-HBP (referred to as v-HBP) using advanced image translation technology can be practically valuable in clinics.

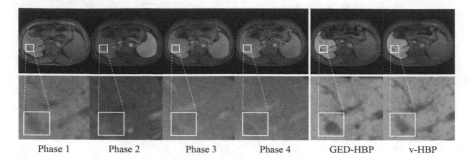

Phase 1   Phase 2   Phase 3   Phase 4   GED-HBP   v-HBP

Fig. 1. A case from our dataset in which the HCC regions are marked with red boxes by radiologists. Phase 1∼4 are 4 phases of DCE-MRIs. HBP and v-HBP are a pair of real and virtual GED-HBP. We can note that misalignment of details exists among all these images.

1.1   Related Works

Image-to-image translation aims to translate images from one domain to another. Deep convolutional generative adversarial networks (DCGAN) [10] produce better training results by replacing a fully connected layer with a fully convolutional layer. Pix2pix is a supervised image-to-image translation model proposed by Isola et al. [6] using a conditional GAN model. Due to the potential unavailability or limited accessibility of paired data in various scenarios, DiscoGAN [7], CycleGAN [23] and DualGAN [20] have been proposed to address the challenging unsupervised image-to-image translation task. However, these methods tend to generate numerous rich but unrealistic details and artifacts.

Generative model for medical image analysis has received a lot of attention recently. However, different from the synthesis of single-class medical images (e.g., brain MRI [19], lesion area patches [5]), liver MRI has multi-class anatomy (i.e., liver, spleen, spine, and so on). Therefore, as illustrated in [22], the attention-aware generator may extract more information specific to the region of interest, which improves the performance of tumor detection. Similar thoughts can be found in TarGAN [3], which incorporate target masks to enable the generator to focus on the local translation of the target area.

A straightforward strategy to construct paired training images is to register these multi-modality MRIs. However, there always exist small misalignments, *i.e.* intra-sequence misalignments among 4-phase DCE-MRIs as well as inter-sequence misalignments between DCE-MRIs and GED-HBP, leading to blurred and corrupted local details which can be critical for assessing pathologies. Arar et al. [1] introduced a multi-modal registration method for natural images, but their work focused only on registration and did not discuss the relationship between registration and image translation. Beyond the above difficulties, the long scanning time of GED-HBP results in minimal liver morphology changes but significant differences in the intestinal region, which might cause more artifacts.

1.2   Contribution

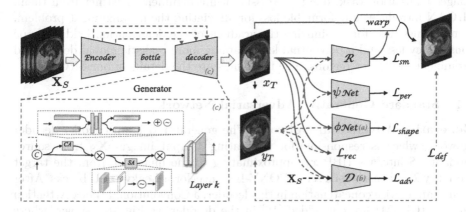

Fig. 2. The framework of our MrGAN method. We use an encoder-decoder model as the generator. $\mathcal{R}$ denotes the auxiliary registration network and ψ Net calculates the perceptual similarity loss. (a) is a pre-trained pseudo-label segmentation network (ϕ Net). (b) is the discriminator of our MrGAN model. (c) presents a CBAM layer in the decoder, where CA and SA denote the channel and spatial attention, respectively.

To address the aforementioned issues, we design MrGAN to efficiently and effectively integrate the information from the 4-phase DCE-MRIs to generate v-HBP. To the best of our knowledge, our work is the first to achieve image translation between different contrast agents using multiple phases of DCE-MRI. We train the generator with an auxiliary registration network that adapts to the intra-sequence and inter-sequence misalignments, thereby seeking the optimal solution for both translation and registration tasks. Since the paired DCE-MRIs and GED-HBP may exhibit minimal changes in liver morphology but significant differences in the intestinal region, our method applies shape consistency through a pre-trained segmentation network, enabling a more prominent local generation in the liver region.

Our contribution is three-fold: 1) We propose a new dataset and a novel application by translating multi-phase DCE-MRIs to generate v-HBP as practical substitutes for GED-HBP. 2) We develop a multi-phase, registration-guided GAN, referred to as MrGAN, which addresses both intra-sequence and inter-sequence misalignments. 3) We validate the proposed MrGAN using clinical data with promising results.

2   Methodology

As depicted in Fig. 2, MrGAN has 4 steps: 1) We use a set of pseudo labels of liver segmentation to train an anatomy network ϕ as shape priors. 2) A generator $\mathcal{G}$ translates multi-phase images input into v-HBP. 3) A discriminator $\mathcal{D}$ ensures good image fidelity and contains the right target characteristics. 4) An auxiliary registration network $\mathcal{R}$ guides the generator to address misalignment problem. Conventional GANs in image-to-image translation (*e.g.* pix2pix [6]) combine reconstruction loss and adversarial loss, but are not effective in this multi-phase images translation task, due to the issue of misalignment. Distinct from them, MrGAN introduces a deformable loss for alleviating the misalignment problem, a smoothness loss for minimizing the gradient of the deformation field, a shape consistency loss and a perceptual loss enabling more realistic global details and prominent local liver regions. The followings are the details of our MrGAN.

2.1   Standard Generative Adversarial Network

Generative Adversarial Network. The generator $\mathcal{G}$ is an encoder-decoder network, which is responsible for translating 4 input images $\mathbf{X}_S$ from source modality S into a v-HBP x_T approximating to the image y_T from the target modality T. $\mathcal{G}$ consists of a set of CONV-InstanceNorm-LeakyReLU blocks. After each channel-wise concatenation in the decoder, a Convolutional Block Attention Module (CBAM) layer is added [18] in the decoder, as Fig. 2(c) shows, where channel attention (CA) and spatial attention (SA) blocks are utilized to facilitate channel-wise and spatial-wise feature recalibration, respectively. $\mathcal{D}$ distinguishes whether the v-HBP is real or fake, as Fig. 2(b) shows. We minimize conditional and patch GAN loss as [6], which leads to higher quality image generation compared to the traditional GAN loss, and define adversarial loss as

$$\min_{\mathcal{G}}\max_{\mathcal{D}}\mathcal{L}_{adv}(\mathcal{G},\mathcal{D}) = \mathbb{E}_{\mathbf{X}_S,y_T}[\log\mathcal{D}(\mathbf{X}_S,y_T)] + \mathbb{E}_{\mathbf{X}_S,y_T}[\log(1-\mathcal{D}(\mathbf{X}_S,\mathcal{G}(\mathbf{X}_S)))]. \quad (1)$$

Reconstruction Loss. As the generator is tasked to not only fool the discriminator but also approximate the ground truth output in an L_1 sense, we use L_1 loss to reconstruct the target image. Furthermore, as our method does not require pixel-level accuracy, a Gaussian blur kernel is incorporated to alleviate the L_1 loss, which is given respectively as

$$\min_{\mathcal{G}}\mathcal{L}_{L_1}(\mathcal{G}) = \mathbb{E}_{\mathbf{X}_S,y_T}[\|y_T - \mathcal{G}(\mathbf{X}_S)\|_1], \min_{\mathcal{G}}\mathcal{L}_{L_1^*}(\mathcal{G}) = \mathbb{E}_{\mathbf{X}_S,y_T}[\|y_T^* - \mathcal{G}(\mathbf{X}_S)^*\|_1], \quad (2)$$

where $G(\mathbf{X}_S)^*$ and y_T^* are blurred $\mathcal{G}(\mathbf{X}_S)$ and y_T, respectively. We add these two loss functions togther as $\mathcal{L}_{rec}(\mathcal{G}) = \mathcal{L}_{L_1}(\mathcal{G}) + \mathcal{L}_{L_1^*}(\mathcal{G})$.

2.2   Registration-Guided Generative Adversarial Network

Beyond the standard GANs, our MrGAN introduces deformation loss, smoothness loss, shape consistency loss, and perceptual loss to address intra-sequence and inter-sequence misalignment issues in multi-phase image translation.

Deformable Registration Network. Inspired by [8], a registration network and GAN are trained simultaneously, in order to alleviate the misalignment problem of intra-sequence and inter-sequence. $\mathcal{R}$ predicts the deformable vector field (DVF) between v-HBP and GED-HBP. Affine registration and a vector momentum-parameterized stationary velocity field (vSVF) are implemented to get better transformation regulation. The registration network is based on U-net [11] and the deformation loss is defined as

$$\min_{\mathcal{G},\mathcal{R}}\mathcal{L}_{def}(\mathcal{G},\mathcal{R}) = \mathbb{E}_{\mathbf{X}_S,y_T}[\|y_T - \mathcal{G}(\mathbf{X}_S) \circ \mathcal{R}(\mathcal{G}(\mathbf{X}_S),y_T)\|_1], \qquad (3)$$

where, $R(G(\mathbf{X}_S),y_T)$ is the deformation field and symbol $\circ$ represents the warp operation. Moreover, a smoothness loss [2] is defined to evaluate the smoothness of the deformation field and minimize its gradient, namely,

$$\min_{\mathcal{R}}\mathcal{L}_{sm}(\mathcal{R}) = \mathbb{E}_{\mathbf{X}_S,y_T}[\|\nabla \mathcal{R}(\mathcal{G}(\mathbf{X}_S),y_T)\|_2^2]. \qquad (4)$$

The smoothness loss regularization can avoid the deformation field from being too large to cause possible foldings or unrealistic details in the output images.

Shape Consistency. Since the long scanning time of GED- HBP results in significant differences in the intestinal region and we pay more attention on the liver region, we add a shape consistency loss [3]. A segmentation network ϕ [11], as shown in Fig. 2(a), is pre-trained to regularize the result into a desired realistic shape and more prominent liver region. The shape consistency loss is defined as

$$\min_{\mathcal{G}}\mathcal{L}_{sp}(\mathcal{G}) = \mathbb{E}_{\mathbf{X}_S,y_T}[\|\phi(\mathcal{G}(\mathbf{X}_S)) - \phi(y_T)\|_2], \qquad (5)$$

where $\phi(\cdot)$ is the feature map of the segmentation network pre-trained.

Perceptual Similarity. The generated images generally suffer from missing fine details in the space [16] with only pixel-wise losses. Perceptual loss [21] is applied for feature-level comparison to provide additional constraints, calculated by extracting the intermediate features of pre-trained VGG-19 as follows,

$$\min_{\mathcal{G}}\mathcal{L}_{per}(\mathcal{G}) = \mathbb{E}_{\mathbf{X}_S,y_T}\sum_l \frac{1}{H_l W_l C_l}\|\psi_l(\mathcal{G}(\mathbf{X}_S)) - \psi_l(y_T)\|_2, \qquad (6)$$

where, $\psi_l(\cdot)$ is the lth layer map of feature extractor.

Finally, we combine all the loss functions above as follows,

$$\min_{\mathcal{G},\mathcal{R}}\max_{\mathcal{D}}\mathcal{L}_{total}(\mathcal{G},\mathcal{R},\mathcal{D}) = \mathcal{L}_{adv} + \lambda_1\mathcal{L}_{rec} + \lambda_2(\mathcal{L}_{def} + \mathcal{L}_{sm}) + \lambda_3\mathcal{L}_{sp} + \lambda_4\mathcal{L}_{per}. \qquad (7)$$

These techniques can result in better translation. The weights, $\lambda_1, \lambda_2, \cdots, \lambda_4$, balance the regularization effect of these techniques.

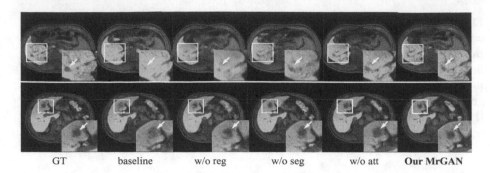

Fig. 3. Ablation study: qualitative results with ground truth (GT) in different settings

Table 1. Ablation study: quantitative results under different settings. To measure image quality, we compute a perceptual metric, *i.e.*, LPIPS [21], between feature maps from GED-HBP and v-HBP. Bold denotes the best performance in terms of mean values.

Methods	Quantitative Metrics			
	MAE ↓	PSNR↑	SSIM↑	LPIPS↓
baseline	0.104 ± 0.037	18.100 ± 2.187	0.632 ± 0.055	0.220 ± 0.042
MrGAN w/o att	0.102 ± 0.040	18.812 ± 2.31	0.671 ± 0.064	0.198 ± 0.046
MrGAN w/o seg	0.103 ± 0.037	18.760 ± 2.152	0.679 ± 0.057	0.199 ± 0.044
MrGAN w/o reg	0.104 ± 0.045	18.581 ± 2.086	0.651 ± 0.054	0.208 ± 0.042
MrGAN	$\mathbf{0.096 \pm 0.035}$	$\mathbf{19.108 \pm 2.134}$	$\mathbf{0.685 \pm 0.065}$	$\mathbf{0.186 \pm 0.045}$

3   Experiments and Results

3.1   Experiments

Dataset. Our dataset of Multi-Phase Liver DCE-MRI images includes 131 patients. These samples were obtained within a month, using conventional Gd-DTPA and Gd-EOB-DTPA agents, and scanned by Siemens 3.0T Skyra or Philips Ingenia 3.0T, consisting of 26 to 78 slices. The dataset includes non-enhanced MR images, hepatic arterial phase, portal venous phase, delayed phase of DCE-MRI, and GED-HBP, as shown in Fig. 1. DCE-MRI and GED-HBP scans were obtained at 0, 25, 60, and 180 s post-injection of Gd-DTPA and at 20 min post-injection of Gd-EOB-DTPA, respectively. Radiologists provided the pathological gold standard for 50 HCC cases.

Data Preprocessing. The dataset underwent intra-subject 3D image registration followed by inter-sequence registration using an affine transformation and multi-scaled FFD [12] transformation to coarsely align the DCE-MRI to the GED-HBP. Due to the limited size of the dataset, we used the validation set as the test set. The proposed dataset was divided into a training and test set with

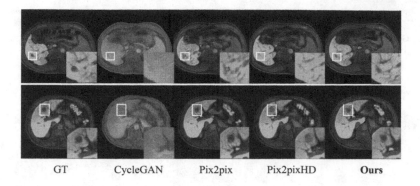

GT   CycleGAN   Pix2pix   Pix2pixHD   **Ours**

Fig. 4. Visualized results of different methods on the task of image translation.

Table 2. Quantitative results of different models on the task of image translation.

Metrics				
Methods	MAE↓	PSNR↑	SSIM↑	LPIPS↓
cycleGAN [23]	0.221 ± 0.039	11.588 ± 0.847	0.182 ± 0.056	0.605 ± 0.027
pix2pix [6]	0.124 ± 0.035	18.080 ± 2.053	0.621 ± 0.054	0.240 ± 0.044
pix2pixHD [17]	0.119 ± 0.034	18.353 ± 1.990	0.625 ± 0.058	0.216 ± 0.034
Our MrGAN	$\mathbf{0.096 \pm 0.035}$	$\mathbf{19.108 \pm 2.134}$	$\mathbf{0.685 \pm 0.065}$	$\mathbf{0.186 \pm 0.045}$

a ratio of 4:1. We expanded the dataset by splitting the 3D volumes into 2D slices, resulting in a total of 2703 slices. All MRIs were resized into 256×256 by resampling to $1 \times 1\ mm^2$. The min-max normalization overcame the intensity differences among subjects and removed the pixels with extreme values. We used data augmentation during training by applying a uniform random affine transformation with elements in the affine matrix sampled from a normal distribution $\mathcal{N}(0, 0.02)$ and a random translation of 5px.

Training. The proposed method is developed on PyTorch and trained on one NVIDIA RTX 2080Ti. We use the Adam optimizer with an initial learning rate of 10^{-4} with momentum parameters of $\beta_1 = 0.5$ and $\beta_2 = 0.999$. The network is trained for 100 epochs with a batch size of 1. We set the loss trade-off hyper-parameters $\lambda_1, \lambda_2, ..., \lambda_4$ to 5, 1, 1, and 0.5, respectively.

3.2   Results

Ablation study. We conducted the ablation experiments to verify the effectiveness of our three key components including the registration network, segmentation network, and attention block. Our experiment settings included: 1) the baseline GAN without three key components (baseline), 2) the MrGAN without attention block (MrGAN w/o att), 3) the MrGAN without segmentation network (MrGAN w/o seg), 4) the MrGAN without registration network (MrGAN

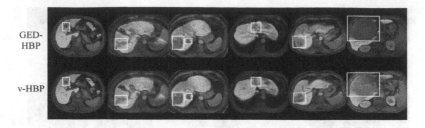

Fig. 5. Clinical evaluation: qualitative results in HCC diagnosis.

w/o reg), and 5) the proposed MrGAN. Figure 3 and Table 1 present both qualitative and quantitative results. Our key components outperformed the baseline method in all measurements, particularly in the lesion regions highlighted by the red boxes. Our registration-guided method also performed better than other components, which was more valid for bypassing the misalignment problem.

As shown in Table 1 and Fig. 3, training with additional modules enhanced edge information and produced more realistic results. The registration network yields a substantial improvement in the qualitative metric. This is because in this setting the registration network R implicitly performs both the alignment tasks. Visual results of v-HBP by MrGAN were most similar to the ground truth, with sharper textures and more details, particularly in red-boxed regions.

Comparison to Image Translation Methods. To demonstrate the superiority of our proposed MrGAN method, we compared our method with three state-of-the-art image translation methods, including CycleGAN, pix2pix, and pix2pixHD [17]. We trained the MrGAN by minimizing the total loss in (7).

Table 3. Results of hypothesis testing. The alternative hypotheses are $H_0^{(1)} : \#\{x_T\} > \#\{y_T\}$, $H_0^{(2)} : \#\{x_T\} < \#\{y_T\}$ and $H_0^{(3)} : \#\{x_T\} \neq \#\{y_T\}$ respectively.

Hypothesis			
Methods ($\alpha = 0.05$)	$H_0^{(1)}$(Greater)	$H_0^{(2)}$ (Less)	$H_0^{(3)}$(Two-sided)
Wilcoxon Rank Sum test (p-value)	0.9703	0.1729	0.3458
Mann-Whitney U test (p-value)	0.9322	0.0823	0.1646
Sign test (p-value)	/	/	0.1250

Table 2 reports the quantitative results of compared methods. One can see that our MrGAN outperforms the other three methods. We showed qualitative results from two HCC patients in Fig. 4. The highlighted demonstrates that our MrGAN method significantly outperforms other methods in the liver area, particularly the lesion area. Instead, other GAN-based methods generated numerous artifacts that are absent in the original image, which hinders radiologists' accurate diagnosis. This suggests MrGAN can not only generate realistic v-HBP but also properly retain liver and lesion structure.

Clinical Evaluation. We greatly focused on the evaluations from radiologists, particularly regarding the performance of the liver region in our results. For the purpose of diagnosis, we performed the Wilcoxon Rank Sum test, Mann Whitney U test, and sign test [4] to test our null hypothesis [14], namely no significant difference between the v-HBP by MrGAN and the GED-HBP in HCC diagnosis.

1) $\#\{x_T\} > \#\{y_T\}$: The v-HBP outperforms the GED-HBP.
2) $\#\{x_T\} = \#\{y_T\}$: There is no significant difference between them.
3) $\#\{x_T\} < \#\{y_T\}$: This is the opposite case of the first hypothesis.

where $\#$ refers to the number of cases in each class. And the resultant p-values with different statistics are shown in Table 3.

Table 3 presents all testing results, meaning that we cannot reject the null hypothesis at a significance level of 0.05. (See examples in the Fig. 5.) This indicates that there is no statistically significant difference between the v-HBP by MrGAN and the GED-HBP in clinical diagnosis.

4 Conclusion

This work introduces a novel application by translating multi-phase DCE-MRIs into a virtual image, toward replacing GED-HBP which is too costly to be widely available in reality. This is achieved via a new framework based on a registration-guided GAN, which addresses the common misalignment problem, and the shape consistency method, which has effectively exploited shape information. Our MrGAN results in more realistic global details and prominent local liver regions in v-HBP. Experimental results also demonstrated that our MrGAN outperformed existing methods in quantitative, qualitative, and clinical metrics. In the future, we plan to explore the potential of the additional clinical diagnostic benefits of generating GED-HBP beyond HCC detection, such as focal nodular hyperplasia(FNH), hepatocellular adenoma(HCA), and so on.

References

1. Arar, M., Ginger, Y., Danon, D., Bermano, A.H., Cohen-Or, D.: Unsupervised multi-modal image registration via geometry preserving image-to-image translation. In: Proceedings of the IEEE/CVF Conference on Computer Vision and Pattern Recognition, pp. 13410–13419 (2020)
2. Balakrishnan, G., Zhao, A., Sabuncu, M.R., Guttag, J., Dalca, A.V.: Voxelmorph: a learning framework for deformable medical image registration. IEEE Trans. Med. Imaging **38**(8), 1788–1800 (2019)
3. Chen, J., Wei, J., Li, R.: TarGAN: target-aware generative adversarial networks for multi-modality medical image translation. In: de Bruijne, M., et al. (eds.) MICCAI 2021. LNCS, vol. 12906, pp. 24–33. Springer, Cham (2021). https://doi.org/10.1007/978-3-030-87231-1_3

4. Conover, W.J.: Practical nonparametric statistics, vol. 350. John wiley & sons (1999)
5. Frid-Adar, M., Diamant, I., Klang, E., Amitai, M., Goldberger, J., Greenspan, H.: Gan-based synthetic medical image augmentation for increased CNN performance in liver lesion classification. Neurocomputing **321**, 321–331 (2018)
6. Isola, P., Zhu, J.-Y., Zhou, T., Efros, A.A.: Image-to-image translation with conditional adversarial networks. In: Proceedings of the IEEE Conference on Computer Vision and Pattern Recognition, pp. 1125–1134 (2017)
7. Kim, T., Cha, M., Kim, H., Lee, J.K., Kim, J.: Learning to discover cross-domain relations with generative adversarial networks. In: International Conference on Machine Learning, pp. 1857–1865. PMLR (2017)
8. Kong, L., Lian, C., Huang, D., Yanle, H., Zhou, Q., Li, Z.: Breaking the dilemma of medical image-to-image translation. Adv. Neural. Inf. Process. Syst. **34**, 1964–1978 (2021)
9. Purysko, A.S., Remer, E.M., Veniero, J.C.: Focal liver lesion detection and characterization with gd-eob-dtpa. Clin. Radiol. **66**(7), 673–684 (2011)
10. Radford, A., Metz, L., Chintala, S.: Unsupervised representation learning with deep convolutional generative adversarial networks. arXiv preprint arXiv:1511.06434 (2015)
11. Ronneberger, O., Fischer, P., Brox, T.: U-Net: convolutional networks for biomedical image segmentation. In: Navab, N., Hornegger, J., Wells, W.M., Frangi, A.F. (eds.) MICCAI 2015. LNCS, vol. 9351, pp. 234–241. Springer, Cham (2015). https://doi.org/10.1007/978-3-319-24574-4_28
12. Rueckert, D., Sonoda, L.I., Hayes, C., Hill, D.L.G., Leach, M.O., Hawkes, D.J.: Nonrigid registration using free-form deformations: application to breast mr images. IEEE Trans. Med. Imaging **18**(8), 712–721 (1999)
13. Sano, K., et al.: Imaging study of early hepatocellular carcinoma: usefulness of gadoxetic acid-enhanced mr imaging. Radiology **261**(3), 834–844 (2011)
14. Shan, H., et al.: Competitive performance of a modularized deep neural network compared to commercial algorithms for low-dose CT image reconstruction. Nat. Mach. Intell. **1**(6), 269–276 (2019)
15. Verloh, N., et al.: Assessing liver function by liver enhancement during the hepatobiliary phase with gd-eob-dtpa-enhanced mri at 3 tesla. Eur. Radiol. **24**, 1013–1019 (2014)
16. Wang, C., Chang, X., Wang, C., Tao, D.: Perceptual adversarial networks for image-to-image transformation. IEEE Trans. Image Process. **27**(8), 4066–4079 (2018)
17. Wang, T.-C., Liu, M.-Y., Zhu, J.-Y., Tao, A., Kautz, J., Catanzaro, B.: High-resolution image synthesis and semantic manipulation with conditional gans. In: Proceedings of the IEEE Conference on Computer Vision and Pattern Recognition, pp. 8798–8807 (2018)
18. Woo, S., Park, J., Lee, J.-Y., Kweon, I.S.: CBAM: convolutional block attention module. In: Ferrari, V., Hebert, M., Sminchisescu, C., Weiss, Y. (eds.) ECCV 2018. LNCS, vol. 11211, pp. 3–19. Springer, Cham (2018). https://doi.org/10.1007/978-3-030-01234-2_1
19. Yang, W., et al.: Predicting CT image from MRI data through feature matching with learned nonlinear local descriptors. IEEE Trans. Med. Imaging **37**(4), 977–987 (2018)
20. Yi, Z., Zhang, H., Tan, P., Gong, M.: Dualgan: unsupervised dual learning for image-to-image translation. In: Proceedings of the IEEE International Conference on Computer Vision, pp. 2849–2857 (2017)

21. Zhang, R., Isola, P., Efros, A.A., Shechtman, E., Wang, O.: The unreasonable effectiveness of deep features as a perceptual metric. In: Proceedings of the IEEE Conference on Computer Vision and Pattern Recognition, pp. 586–595 (2018)
22. Zhao, J., et al.: Tripartite-gan: synthesizing liver contrast-enhanced mri to improve tumor detection. Med. Image Anal. **63**, 101667 (2020)
23. Zhu, J.-Y., Park, T., Isola, P., Efros, A.A.: Unpaired image-to-image translation using cycle-consistent adversarial networks. In: Proceedings of the IEEE International Conference on Computer Vision, pp. 2223–2232 (2017)

Learned Local Attention Maps
for Synthesising Vessel Segmentations
from T2 MRI

Yash Deo[1(✉)], Rodrigo Bonazzola[1], Haoran Dou[1], Yan Xia[1], Tianyou Wei[1], Nishant Ravikumar[1,2], Alejandro F. Frangi[1,2,3,4,5], and Toni Lassila[1,2]

[1] Centre for Computational Imaging and Simulation Technologies in Biomedicine (CISTIB), School of Computing and School of Medicine, University of Leeds, Leeds, UK
sc19ynpd@leeds.ac.uk
[2] NIHR Leeds Biomedical Research Centre (BRC), Leeds, UK
[3] Alan Turing Institute, London, UK
[4] Medical Imaging Research Center (MIRC), Electrical Engineering and Cardiovascular Sciences Departments, KU Leuven, Leuven, Belgium
[5] Division of Informatics, Imaging and Data Science, Schools of Computer Science and Health Sciences, University of Manchester, Manchester, UK

Abstract. Magnetic resonance angiography (MRA) is an imaging modality for visualising blood vessels. It is useful for several diagnostic applications and for assessing the risk of adverse events such as haemorrhagic stroke (resulting from the rupture of aneurysms in blood vessels). However, MRAs are not acquired routinely, hence, an approach to synthesise blood vessel segmentations from more routinely acquired MR contrasts such as T1 and T2, would be useful. We present an encoder-decoder model for synthesising segmentations of the main cerebral arteries in the circle of Willis (CoW) from only T2 MRI. We propose a two-phase multi-objective learning approach, which captures both global and local features. It uses learned local attention maps generated by dilating the segmentation labels, which forces the network to only extract information from the T2 MRI relevant to synthesising the CoW. Our synthetic vessel segmentations generated from only T2 MRI achieved a mean Dice score of 0.79 ± 0.03 in testing, compared to state-of-the-art segmentation networks such as transformer U-Net (0.71 ± 0.04) and nnU-net(0.68 ± 0.05), while using only a fraction of the parameters. The main qualitative difference between our synthetic vessel segmentations and the comparative models was in the sharper resolution of the CoW vessel segments, especially in the posterior circulation.

Keywords: Image Synthesis · Deep Learning · Brain Vasculature · Vessel Segmentation · Multi-modal Imaging

1 Introduction

A magnetic resonance angiogram (MRA) contains vital information for visualising the brain vasculature, which includes an anastomotic ring of arteries located

© The Author(s), under exclusive license to Springer Nature Switzerland AG 2023
J. M. Wolterink et al. (Eds.): SASHIMI 2023, LNCS 14288, pp. 32–41, 2023.
https://doi.org/10.1007/978-3-031-44689-4_4

at the base of the brain called the circle of Willis (CoW). Multiple different topological variants of the CoW exist in the general population, and certain variants of the CoW can lead to worse outcomes following a stroke [12]. To that end, it would be useful to visualise the main cerebral blood vessels in large imaging datasets and identify them by CoW phenotype to understand their relevance to stroke in the general population. Vessel segmentation from MRA is a well-studied problem with state-of-the-art methods achieving high quality vessel segmentation results [13] with Dice scores as high as 0.91 [20]. However, as MRA acquisition may require the injection of contrast agents and has longer acquisition times, it is not commonly available in population imaging studies. T1- and T2-weighted MRI scans are the most common MR imaging modalities available and are used to study the presence of lesions or other abnormal structures in the brain. While the blood vessels are not explicitly visible in these modalities, they contain latent information that can be used to synthesise the major vessels in the brain.

Generative adversarial neural networks [4] (GANNs) have seen remarkable success in the field of image synthesis, with networks like pix2pix [9] achieving impressive results in paired image-to-image synthesis. GANNs have also been widely used in medical image synthesis in various use cases such as generating T1, T2, and FLAIR images of the brain using Wasserstein-GANNs [5]. Progressively growing GANNs [1] have been used for the generation of retinal fundus and brain images. Previous works on brain MRA synthesis used SGAN [17] to generate MRA from paired T1 and T2 images, or used starGAN [19] to synthesise MRA given T1, T2 and/or a PD-weighted MRI as input. GANN-based approaches such as vox2vox [3] have been used to synthesise segmentations of brain tumour directly from T1, T2, Gadolinium-enhanced T1, and T2 FLAIR modalities. Most GANN based approaches synthesise MRA from multiple other MR modalities, and then require the use of a separate segmentation algorithm, such as U-net (which is popularly accepted as baseline), to segment the brain vascular structures from the synthesised MRA. As the brain vessels form a very small portion of the MRA image, attention mechanisms were introduced to the segmentation algorithms to more accurately capture the small vessels. This has been achieved in networks such as Attention U-Net [16] or more recently transformer based networks such as TransU-Net [2].

In spite of their successes, GANs and transformers are complex models with tens or hundreds of millions of parameters that can be notoriously hard to train. On top of that, GANNs tend to produce phantoms (non-existent image features), especially when dealing with very high-resolution images with intrinsic detail arising from medical imaging [21]. To alleviate these issues, we propose multi-task learnable localised attention maps to directly generate vessel segmentations based on a U-Net architecture, which can capture both global and local features from the input domain. Our method requires only the T2 modality as in input, which eliminates the need of multiple input modalities. The learned local attention maps enable the trained model to only look for vessels in specific parts of the image, which drastically decreases the number of parameters required to train the synthesis network. Our model consequently synthesises more accurate CoW segmentations with fewer parameters than competing GANN-based approaches.

2   Methodology

We propose a deep convolutional encoder-decoder model, which is trained with two-phase multi-task learning. At training time, paired T2 images and ground-truth MRA segmentations are available. Our encoder-decoder network captures both global information (by encoding input images into a latent space) and local information (by learning soft attention maps for brain vessels based on MRA segmentations) from the given input images. We train the model using multi-task learning in two phases, where a learned local attention map learns where on the T2 image the vessels are most likely located to improve the synthesised vessel segmentation masks. At run-time, the model efficiently synthesises brain vessel segmentation masks from only T2 images.

2.1   Data and Pre-processing

The model was trained on the IXI dataset [7] using the 3T scans acquired at Hammersmith Hospital, and includes paired T2 and MRA scans of 181 patients. The T2 and MRA images were first registered using rigid registration. The images were centered, cropped from 512×512 to 400×400, and intensity-normalised. Ground-truth segmentations were then generated from the MRA images for each corresponding T2 slice using a residual U-Net [11]. The segmentations were then dilated to form a binary mask and multiplied pixelwise with the corresponding T2 slice to create the ground truth local attention map (see Fig. 1)

2.2   Network Architecture

The proposed model follows the general architecture of the pix2pix-model [9] with one encoder branch and two output branches (Fig. 3). The encoder branch combines U-net and Resnet [6] architectures with a latent space consisting of three consecutive residual blocks, similar to the vox2vox-model [3]. The encoder has four convolution + max-pooling -blocks, where each block consists of three strided convolution layers followed by a max-pooling layer. Each convolution layer is followed by an instance-normalisation -layer. The latent space branches out into two output branches: the decoding branch and the synthesis branch. In case of multiple input modalities (eg. T1 + T2) we have a separate decoding branch for each modality. The output branches have the same structure as the encoding branch with the max-pooling layers replaced by up-sampling layers and with skip connections from corresponding encoding blocks. The first convolution block of the synthesis branch receives a skip connection from both the corresponding encoder branch and the decoder branch.

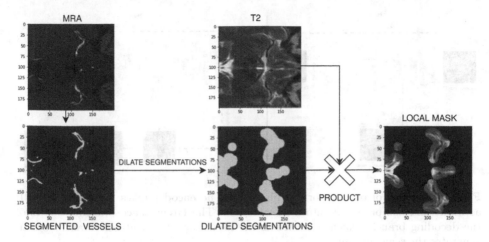

Fig. 1. Process for the generation of the local attention masks. Vessel segmentations are generated from the MRA and dilated. We then multiply this dilation with the corresponding T2 slice to create the mask.

Local Attention Mask. The output of the segmentation branch consists of fine vessel information. The small dimensions of the vessels make the segmentation masks unsuitable for generating the local attention maps. For this reason, we dilate these vessel segments to 10 pixels in each direction to create a local attention mask. The optimal dilation width was found through experimentation as shown in Table 1. We then perform pixel-wise multiplication of this local attention mask with the output of the decoder to generate a local attention map as shown in Fig. 1. This local attention map is compared to the ground truth local attention maps during model training to calculate loss. This dependency between these two tasks adds a collaborative element between what would otherwise be two contrastive tasks. The use of a local attention mask forces the network to learn from a very small portion of the input image, which contains information about the blood vessels and ignore the rest of the image. This property allows us to greatly reduce the number of parameters required to train the model.

2.3   Training and Losses

The network is trained in two phases to effectively capture both the global and local features required to synthesise the vessels from T2 images (Fig. 2).

Phase 1: We pre-train the network on T2 images by freezing the synthesis branch and only training the decoder branch, effectively training an autoencoder for T2 images. The network is trained with an early stopping criteria based on the loss slope. The only loss calculated in this stage is the T2 reconstruction loss from the decoder branch. The loss function used is L1 and is specified below where X_{T_2} is the ground truth T2 image and $\hat{X}_{T_2}$ is the generated T2 image:

$$\mathcal{L}_{\text{phase 1}} = \text{MAE}(X_{T_2}, \hat{X}_{T_2}) \tag{1}$$

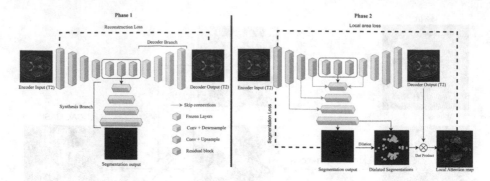

Fig. 2. Overview of our network architecture. The encoder takes T2-weighted MRI as input and compresses it into a latent space. The latent space branches out into the decoding branch, which reconstructs the input, and the synthesis branch, which generates the segmentation.

Phase 2: After we finish the pre-training step, we unfreeze the synthesis branch and train it in conjunction with the decoder branch. Although the decoder branch is being trained in this step, the loss calculated for this branch is not the reconstruction loss but local loss, which is calculated over the dot product of the output of the decoder branch and the dilated segmentation obtained from the output of the synthesis branch.

In order to train these two contrasting branches together, we tested our model with various multi-task learning (MTL) approaches: Nash-MTL [15] (average Dice after evaluation 0.76), CAGrad [14] (average Dice after evaluation 0.74), and uncertainty-based MTL =[10] (average Dice after evaluation 0.79). The best performing version was the uncertainty-based MTL, where both the losses are weighted based on the assumption of homoscedastic uncertainty for each task. The loss function for our multi-output model is described in (2), where W are the model parameters and we interpret minimising the loss with respect to σ_1 and σ_2 as learning the relative weights for the losses $\mathcal{L}_{\text{seg}}$ and $\mathcal{L}_{\text{loc}}$ adaptively. We used Dice score as the loss for $\mathcal{L}_{\text{seg}}$ and MAE as the loss for $\mathcal{L}_{\text{loc}}$

$$\mathcal{L}_{\text{phase 2}} = \frac{1}{2\sigma_1^2}\mathcal{L}_{\text{seg}}(\mathbf{W}) + \frac{1}{2\sigma_2^2}\mathcal{L}_{\text{loc}}(\mathbf{W}) + \log \sigma_1\sigma_2 \qquad (2)$$

3   Experiments and Results

3.1   Implementation Details

All the models were implemented in TensorFlow 2.8 and Pytorch (for nnU-Net) and Python 3. Out of the 181 cases in the dataset we used 150 for training and 31 for testing and validation. All the models were pre-trained on T2 images and grid search was used to optimise the following hyperparameters: (1) batch size, (2) learning rate, (3) number of epochs, and (4) momentum. To train the transformer network, we first used the parameters recommended in [2] and applied further fine-tuning of the parameters to achieve comparative performance in the segmentation task.

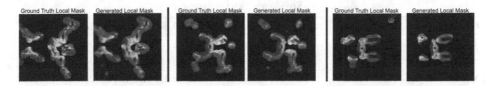

Fig. 3. Local attention maps learned by the network compared against the ground truth local attention maps.

To evaluate the results of our model against other methods, we used the segmentation metrics of Dice score and Hausdorff distance (hd95). The results were averaged over the 3D volumes of the 11 leave-out cases and are shown in Table 2. Our method clearly outperforms conventional GANN-based synthesis methods, such as vox2vox, and also performs slightly better than state-of-the-art segmentation models like transformer U-Net [2] and nnU-net [8], while also being easier to train with fewer trainable parameters. We experimented with training our model with different input modalities, which showed that using only T1 as an input had the worst performance (average dice 0.64 ±0.04) while the performance of using only T2 (average dice 0.79 ±0.04) and both T1 + T2 (average dice 0.78 ±0.05) was essentially the same, with T1 + T2 requiring additional parameters (33.4 million) compared to using just T2 (26.7 million) as we would need an additional decoding branch for the T1 decoder. A crucial hyperparameter in our model is the dilation width of the segmentations to generate the local attention maps, which was optimised in a separate experiment. (Table 1).

3.2   Qualitative Results

Figure 4 shows a qualitative comparison of our method against pix2pix, vox2vox, U-Net, nnU-net, and transformer U-Net for two samples from the unseen test

Table 1. Difference in loss with different values of dilation for the local attention mask

Attention mechanism used	Dice (95% CI)	Area covered by mask
No local attention mask	0.62 ± 0.04	NA
Mask with no dilation	0.59 ± 0.04	1.5%
Mask with dilation by 5 pixels	0.74 ± 0.03	8.5%
Mask with dilation by 10 pixels	0.79 ± 0.03	18%
Mask with dilation by 15 pixels	0.75 ± 0.02	28%
Mask with dilation by 20 pixels	0.75 ± 0.03	37%

Table 2. Accuracy of synthesised vessel segmentation masks in a test set of 11 leave-out cases

Model	Model params. ($\times 10^6$)	Dice (95% CI)	HD95 (95% CI)	Model Type
Our model	26.7	0.79 ± 0.03	9.1 ± 0.5	Segmentation/synthesis
Transformer U-Net [2]	105.8	0.71 ± 0.04	10.4 ± 0.5	Segmentation
nnU-Net [8]	127.8	0.68 ± 0.03	9.3 ± 0.4	Segmentation
Vox2vox [3]	78.8	0.67 ± 0.05	17.2 ± 1.4	Segmentation/synthesis
Pix2pix [9]	36.9	0.55 ± 0.04	23.1 ± 3.0	Synthesis
U-Net [18] (base)	9.1	0.57 ± 0.05	42.6 ± 4.2	Segmentation

set. It can be observed that pix2pix and the base U-Net are only able to capture the overall structure of the CoW with a lot of noise. The vox2vox model synthesises the vessels slightly better, but is still unable to capture the finer details and suffers from noise. The nnU-net and transformer U-Net are able to synthesise the vessels with high quality, but struggle to synthesise smaller vessels such as the posterior communicating arteries (PComA) in the first case. An interesting observation can be made in the second case, where the ground truth has faults in the segmentation (especially in the posterior circulation). The Transformer U-Net, nnU-net, and our model attempt to fix these faults by synthesising a continuous PCA, but our model does better in restoring vessel continuity. Figure 5 shows the CoW synthesis results for the best case, worst case, and median case scenarios. It can be observed that in the worst case the model struggles to synthesise the smaller vessels towards the end of the posterior cerebral circulation, whereas in the median case scenario most of the major vessels are synthesised with only the small PComA artery missing. The best case is that all the major arteries of the CoW are synthesised while also removing noise from the input image.

3.3 Limitations

While our method outperforms state-of-the-art approaches with a much smaller number of trainable parameters and is able to generated the complete structure of the CoW, it can be seen that in come cases the model can struggle to generate some of the finer vessels branching from the main arteries (especially the posterior communicating arteries). This could be either because the input data is of insufficient resolution (T2 images were acquired at 3T) or because the T2 modality does not contain information that could be used to synthesise the anterior circulation. It is possible that additional MR modalities, such as multi-view T1, or a fully-3D neural network architecture could add more information about the posterior and anterior vessels and recover a complete CoW.

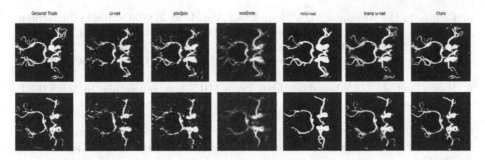

Fig. 4. CoW synthesis results compared between models. Pix2pix and U-Net are able to capture the overall structure of the Cow but with a lot of noise. Vox2vox performs comparatively better, but still suffers from noise in the outputs. NnU-Net, Transformer U-Net and our method show good results with our method capturing more details and dealing better with noise.

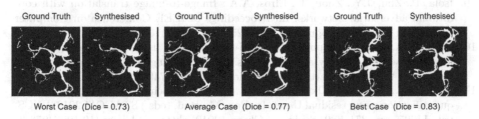

Fig. 5. CoW synthesis results for the average case, the best case, and the worst case in our unseen test set.

4 Conclusion

We proposed a multi-output encoder-decoder -based network that learned to effectively synthesise vessels from only T2-weighted MRI using local attention maps and multi-task learning. The qualitative and quantitative results show that our method outperformed both the state-of-the-art and conventional segmentation/synthesis algorithms, while at the same time being easier to train with fewer parameters. In future work, we are extending our model to a fully 3D synthesis model to achieve better connectivity of the CoW structure.

Acknowledgement. This research was partially supported by the National Institute for Health and Care Research (NIHR) Leeds Biomedical Research Centre (BRC) and the Royal Academy of Engineering Chair in Emerging Technologies (CiET1919/19).

References

1. Beers, A., et al.: High-resolution medical image synthesis using progressively grown generative adversarial networks. arXiv preprint arXiv:1805.03144 (2018)
2. Chen, J., et al.: Transunet: transformers make strong encoders for medical image segmentation. arXiv preprint arXiv:2102.04306 (2021)

3. Cirillo, M.D., Abramian, D., Eklund, A.: Vox2Vox: 3D-GAN for brain tumour segmentation. In: Crimi, A., Bakas, S. (eds.) BrainLes 2020. LNCS, vol. 12658, pp. 274–284. Springer, Cham (2021). https://doi.org/10.1007/978-3-030-72084-1_25
4. Goodfellow, I., et al.: Generative adversarial networks. Commun. ACM **63**(11), 139–144 (2020)
5. Han, C., et al.: GAN-based synthetic brain MR image generation. In: 2018 IEEE International Symposium on Biomedical Imaging (ISBI 2018), pp. 734–738. IEEE (2018)
6. He, K., Zhang, X., Ren, S., Sun, J.: Deep residual learning for image recognition. In: Proc. IEEE Conference on Computer Vision and Pattern Recognition, pp. 770–778 (2016)
7. Information eXtraction from Images Consortium: IXI dataset - brain development. www.brain-development.org/ixi-dataset/, (Accessed 14 Feb 2023)
8. Isensee, F., Jaeger, P.F., Kohl, S.A., Petersen, J., Maier-Hein, K.H.: nnU-Net: a self-configuring method for deep learning-based biomedical image segmentation. Nat. Methods **18**(2), 203–211 (2021)
9. Isola, P., Zhu, J.Y., Zhou, T., Efros, A.A.: Image-to-image translation with conditional adversarial networks. In: Proceedings of IEEE Conference on Computer Vision and Pattern Recognition, pp. 1125–1134 (2017)
10. Kendall, A., Gal, Y., Cipolla, R.: Multi-task learning using uncertainty to weigh losses for scene geometry and semantics. In: Proceedings of IEEE Conference on Computer Vision and Pattern Recognition, pp. 7482–7491 (2018)
11. Kerfoot, E., Clough, J., Oksuz, I., Lee, J., King, A.P., Schnabel, J.A.: Left-ventricle quantification using residual U-net. In: Pop, M., et al. (eds.) STACOM 2018. LNCS, vol. 11395, pp. 371–380. Springer, Cham (2019). https://doi.org/10.1007/978-3-030-12029-0_40
12. Lin, E., Kamel, H., Gupta, A., RoyChoudhury, A., Girgis, P., Glodzik, L.: Incomplete circle of Willis variants and stroke outcome. Eur. J. Radiol. **153**, 110383 (2022)
13. Lin, F., Xia, Y., Song, S., Ravikumar, N., Frangi, A.F.: High-throughput 3dra segmentation of brain vasculature and aneurysms using deep learning. Comput. Methods Programs Biomed. **230**, 107355 (2023) https://doi.org/10.1016/j.cmpb.2023.107355, https://www.sciencedirect.com/science/article/pii/S0169260723000226
14. Liu, B., Liu, X., Jin, X., Stone, P., Liu, Q.: Conflict-averse gradient descent for multi-task learning. Adv. Neural. Inf. Process. Syst. **34**, 18878–18890 (2021)
15. Navon, A., et al.: Multi-task learning as a bargaining game. arXiv preprint arXiv:2202.01017 (2022)
16. Oktay, O., et al.: Attention U-net: learning where to look for the pancreas. arXiv preprint arXiv:1804.03999 (2018)
17. Olut, S., Sahin, Y.H., Demir, U., Unal, G.: Generative adversarial training for MRA image synthesis using multi-contrast MRI. In: Rekik, I., Unal, G., Adeli, E., Park, S.H. (eds.) PRIME 2018. LNCS, vol. 11121, pp. 147–154. Springer, Cham (2018). https://doi.org/10.1007/978-3-030-00320-3_18
18. Ronneberger, O., Fischer, P., Brox, T.: U-Net: convolutional networks for biomedical image segmentation. In: Navab, N., Hornegger, J., Wells, W.M., Frangi, A.F. (eds.) MICCAI 2015. LNCS, vol. 9351, pp. 234–241. Springer, Cham (2015). https://doi.org/10.1007/978-3-319-24574-4_28
19. Sohail, M., Riaz, M.N., Wu, J., Long, C., Li, S.: Unpaired multi-contrast MR image synthesis using generative adversarial networks. In: Burgos, N., Gooya, A., Svoboda, D. (eds.) SASHIMI 2019. LNCS, vol. 11827, pp. 22–31. Springer, Cham (2019). https://doi.org/10.1007/978-3-030-32778-1_3

20. Xiao, R., et al.: Segmentation of cerebrovascular anatomy from TOF-MRA using length-strained enhancement and random walker. Biomed. Res. Int. **2020**, 9347215 (2020)
21. Yu, B., Wang, Y., Wang, L., Shen, D., Zhou, L.: Medical image synthesis via deep learning. In: Lee, G., Fujita, H. (eds.) Deep Learning in Medical Image Analysis. AEMB, vol. 1213, pp. 23–44. Springer, Cham (2020). https://doi.org/10.1007/978-3-030-33128-3_2

Physics-Aware Motion Simulation For T2*-Weighted Brain MRI

Hannah Eichhorn[1,2(✉)], Kerstin Hammernik[2], Veronika Spieker[1,2], Samira M. Epp[3,4], Daniel Rueckert[2,3,5], Christine Preibisch[3], and Julia A. Schnabel[1,2,6]

[1] Institute of Machine Learning in Biomedical Imaging, Helmholtz Munich, Neuherberg, Germany
hannah.eichhorn@helmholtz-munich.de
[2] School of Computation, Information and Technology, Technical University of Munich, Munich, Germany
[3] School of Medicine, Technical University of Munich, Munich, Germany
[4] Graduate School of Systemic Neurosciences, Ludwig-Maximilians-University, Munich, Germany
[5] Department of Computing, Imperial College London, London, UK
[6] School of Biomedical Engineering and Imaging Sciences, King's College London, London, UK

Abstract. In this work, we propose a realistic, physics-aware motion simulation procedure for T_2*-weighted magnetic resonance imaging (MRI) to improve learning-based motion correction. As T_2*-weighted MRI is highly sensitive to motion-related changes in magnetic field inhomogeneities, it is of utmost importance to include physics information in the simulation. Additionally, current motion simulations often only assume simplified motion patterns. Our simulations, on the other hand, include real recorded subject motion and realistic effects of motion-induced magnetic field inhomogeneity changes. We demonstrate the use of such simulated data by training a convolutional neural network to detect the presence of motion in affected k-space lines. The network accurately detects motion-affected k-space lines for simulated displacements down to ≥ 0.5 mm (accuracy on test set: 92.5%). Finally, our results demonstrate exciting opportunities of simulation-based k-space line detection combined with more powerful reconstruction methods. Our code is publicly available at: https://github.com/HannahEichhorn/T2starLineDet.

Keywords: Brain MRI · Motion Artefacts · Motion Detection · Motion Correction · Deep Learning

1 Introduction

T_2* quantification, as part of the multi-parametric quantitative BOLD (mqBOLD) protocol [9], enables oxygenation sensitive brain magnetic resonance

Supplementary Information The online version contains supplementary material available at https://doi.org/10.1007/978-3-031-44689-4_5.

imaging (MRI) and is more affordable and less invasive than positron emission tomography techniques. Quantitative MRI, as opposed to the more widely used qualitative structural imaging, allows for a consistent extraction of biomarkers across scanners and hospitals by measuring physical tissue properties. Promising applications of the quantitative mqBOLD technique comprise stroke, glioma and internal carotid artery stenosis [6,12,19]. Motion artefacts, however, remain a major challenge for brain MRI in general. Specifically, T_2*-weighted gradient echo (GRE) MRI, shows a high sensitivity towards magnetic field (B_0) inhomogeneities and is hence particularly affected by subject head motion [16]. Due to the increasing impact of motion with increasing echo times, motion severely affects the signal decay over several echoes and, thus, the accuracy of the T_2* quantification from multi-echo data [17]. Artefacts have been shown to propagate from the T_2* mapping towards derived parameters even for mild motion with less than 1 mm average displacements during the scans [5], which underlines the need of intra-scan motion correction (MoCo) for T_2*-weighted GRE data.

Deep learning solutions have shown promising results for correcting motion in various MR applications. MoCo has been approached as an image denoising problem, using convolutional neural networks [3,24] as well as generative adversarial networks [11,14]. However, acting purely on image data, such methods cannot guarantee consistency with the acquired raw k-space data, which might hinder their translation into clinical practice. Enforcing data consistency is only possible when combining MoCo with the image reconstruction process [8,18,20]. Yet, the majority of learning-based MoCo techniques - whether purely image-based or combined with the reconstruction process - rely on the availability of paired motion-free and motion-corrupted data for supervised model training [22]. Since the acquisition of large paired datasets is expensive and not always feasible, motion simulation is widely used. However, realistic and physics-aware simulations are still underutilised. Some authors merely exchange k-space lines between different time points [18]. Others use MR physics as basis for a more realistic simulation, but only combine a small number of discrete motion states, ignoring the continuous nature of real subject motion [3,11,20,24]; or only simulate in-plane motion instead of realistic 3D motion [3,20]. Furthermore, second-order motion effects like motion-induced magnetic field changes are commonly ignored.

In this work, we propose a physics-aware motion simulation procedure that allows for more realistic model training in the presence of magnetic field inhomogeneities and demonstrate its use for the learning-based detection of motion-corrupted k-space lines in T2*-weighted MRI. Our contributions are three-fold:

1. We carry out realistic motion simulations based on real recorded patient motion. In contrast to state-of-the-art methods, we do not only include rigid-body transformations, but also B_0 inhomogeneities as second-order effects.
2. Inspired by the work of Oksuz et al. [18], we train a 3D convolutional neural network to classify individual motion-affected k-space lines, leveraging the multi-echo information of the T_2*-weighted brain dataset.
3. To demonstrate the potential of our work, we show motion corrected images where information on motion-affected lines is included as a weighting mask in the data consistency term of the iterative reconstruction procedure.

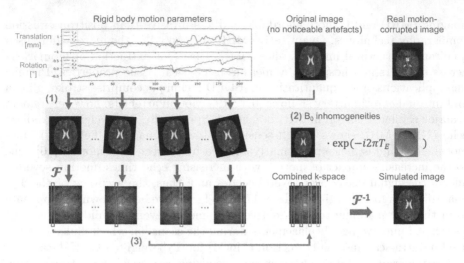

Fig. 1. Visualisation of the motion simulation approach. (1) Rigid-body transformations are applied to the complex original image data for each time point. (2) A phase term with randomly generated B_0 inhomogeneities is multiplied to the transformed images. The results are transformed into k-space. (3) k-Space lines from the individual motion states are merged into the final simulated k-space, accounting for the multi-slice acquisition scheme. An inverse Fourier transform yields the motion corrupted image.

2   Methods

2.1   Motion Simulation

The MRI single coil forward model in the presence of rigid-body motion includes the Fourier transform $\mathcal{F}$, the sampling mask $\mathbf{M}_t$, incorporating the line-wise k-space acquisition pattern, and the three parameter rotation and translation transforms, $\mathbf{R}_t$ and $\mathbf{T}_t$, which are applied to the motion-free image x for each time point t, yielding the motion-affected k-space data y [1]:

$$y = \sum_{t=1}^{T} \mathbf{M}_t \mathcal{F} \mathbf{T}_t \mathbf{R}_t x. \tag{1}$$

As second-order motion effect, we further include a phase shift, which is induced by position-dependent magnetic field inhomogeneities $\omega_{B_0 t}$ and increases with the echo time T_E:

$$y = \sum_{t=1}^{T} \mathbf{M}_t \mathcal{F} e^{-2i\pi\omega_{B_0 t} T_E} \mathbf{T}_t \mathbf{R}_t x. \tag{2}$$

Based on this, motion is simulated by rigidly transforming the complex MRI data and subsequently merging different motion states in k-space, as visualised in Fig. 1. In this process, the actual multi-slice acquisition scheme is considered, i.e. the ordering of phase encoding lines is included in $\mathbf{M}_t$. Additionally, for time points with average displacements of more than 0.5 mm, magnetic field inhomogeneities are incorporated by multiplying the image with a B_0 map that was modified by adding random image gradients with deviations of max. 5 Hz [15].

Motion simulation is only performed for phase encoding (PE) lines, where the average displacement of points within a sphere with radius 64 mm, as model of the head, exceeds a certain threshold value d_{min}. To investigate the amount of motion that can be detected, this so-called *simulation threshold* is varied between 0.25 mm and 1.0 mm in the experiments. To avoid the need of registration for calculating full-reference metrics with respect to the original motion-free image, the motion curves are transformed in a way that the median motion state - measured by the average displacement - is in the zero-position.

2.2   K-Space Line Classification Network

The line classification network takes as input motion corrupted k-space data and predicts a classification label for each PE line (0 or 1 for the presence or absence of motion). The network structure is adapted from Oksuz et al. [18] and consists of five repetitions of 3D convolution, batch normalisation, ReLU activation, dropout and max pooling layers, followed by a fully connected, a dropout and a sigmoid activation layer, as visualised in Fig. S1 of the Supplementary Material. Convolution layers are implemented with a kernel size of $3 \times 3 \times 3$. Max pooling is performed in all dimensions except the PE dimension. The network is trained for 300 epochs with Adam [13] using a learning rate of 5×10^{-4} and a weighted cross entropy loss between prediction m^{pr} and target m^{ta} classification labels:

$$L(m^{pr}, m^{ta}) = -m^{ta} \log(m^{pr} + \epsilon) - \omega \cdot (1 - m^{ta}) \log((1 - m^{pr}) + \epsilon). \quad (3)$$

Weights of the epoch with the lowest validation loss are used. Batch sizes of 32 and 64, weighting factors, ω, between 1 and 5, weight decays between 1×10^{-5} and 5×10^{-2} and dropout probabilities between 10% and 30% are tested and the best configuration is chosen based on the validation dataset (64/5 / 1×10^{-3}/20%; 219,380 trainable parameters). The average runtime of the network training is 14 h. Computations are performed on an NVIDIA RTX A6000, using Python 3.8.12 and PyTorch 1.13.0 (code available at: https://github.com/HannahEichhorn/T2starLineDet).

2.3   Data

Motion simulation for training and evaluation of the line classification network is performed on 116 complex, coil-combined T_2*-weighted datasets of 59 healthy volunteers, which can be expected to not considerably move during the scanning. Two experienced researchers (CP, HE) visually confirmed that these data did not show noticeable motion artefacts. The unpublished mqBOLD data originates from four ongoing studies investigating brain oxygen metabolism on a 3T Philips Elition MR scanner (Philips Healthcare, Best, The Netherlands), using a multi-slice GRE sequence (12 echoes, 30-36 slices, TE1/ΔTE = 5/5 ms, TR=1910-2291 ms, $\alpha = 30°$, voxel size: $2 \times 2 \times 3$ mm^3). The ongoing studies have been approved by the local ethics committee (approval numbers 472/16 S, 446/21 S, 165/21 S, 382/18 S). The available datasets are divided subject-wise into train, validation and test sets (74/18/24 datasets).

For a realistic motion simulation, we base our simulation on real head motion. We extract 132 motion curves of length 235 s from 62 functional MRI (fMRI) time series (unpublished data from two ongoing studies with approval numbers 472/16 S and 15/20 S, independent cohorts from above imaging cohorts). These are divided into train, validation and test sets ($N = 88/20/24$ motion curves), keeping the amount of motion, determined by average and maximum voxel displacement and motion-free time, as equal as possible in the different sets. Principal component analysis is used to determine the largest modes of variations of the training motion curves $pc_i(t)$, which are combined with random weights α_i and added to the mean curve $\overline{T(t)}$ to generate augmented training samples [4]:

$$T_{new}(t) = \overline{T(t)} + \sum_{i=1}^{0.2 \cdot N} \alpha_i \cdot pc_i(t). \tag{4}$$

For each complex image in the training set, six motion curves are generated for simulation. Slices with more than 30% background voxels are excluded. This results in a total of 8,922 slices for training, 392 for validation and 492 for testing.

Preprocessing: The complex data are normalised for each line individually:

$$y_{epr}^{n} = \frac{y_{epr}}{\sqrt{\sum_{ep} | y_{epr} |^2}}, \tag{5}$$

with e, p and r indicating the echo, phase encoding and readout dimension. Real and imaginary parts are fed into the network as different channels.

The target classification labels are calculated by thresholding and inverting the average displacement of a sphere with a 64 mm radius at the acquisition time of the corresponding PE line, using the simulation threshold value d_{min}. The target masks are averaged across all 12 echoes, since these have been acquired within 60 ms and are thus assumed to have been acquired during the same motion state.

2.4   Evaluation

The predicted classification labels are evaluated based on accuracy, corresponding to the rate of correctly predicted lines. For a more detailed interpretation, the rate of non-detected lines (ND) is calculated as the fraction of lines with motion ($m^{ta} = 0$), which the network does not detect ($m^{pr} = 1$). Similarly, the rate of wrongly-detected lines (WD) is calculated as the fraction of lines without motion ($m^{ta} = 1$), which the network classifies as motion-corrupted ($m^{pr} = 0$).

2.5   Weighted Iterative Reconstruction

Inspired by the work of Jiang et al. [10], we include the estimated motion classification as weights into the data consistency (DC) term of the single coil MRI

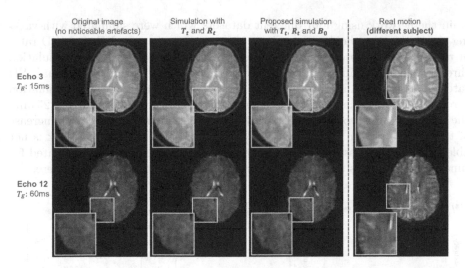

Fig. 2. Example images showing the relevance of B_0 inhomogeneities for generating realistic artefact patterns. From left to right: original images (without noticeable motion artefacts), simulated images without and with B_0 inhomogeneities and real motion images for two different echo times (top and bottom row). The motion curve for the simulation is shown in Fig. S2 of the Supplementary Material (mean displacement during the whole scan: 0.89 mm, simulation threshold: 0.5 mm). Artefacts - i.e. blurring of underlying structures and wave-like patterns - are more pronounced for the later echo in the real motion case and in the proposed simulation method, while the early echo is not significantly affected by such mild motion.

reconstruction model with total variation (TV) regularisation:

$$x^* = \arg \min_x \frac{1}{2} \parallel \mathbf{W}(\mathbf{A}x - y) \parallel_2^2 + \lambda \parallel \boldsymbol{\Phi}x \parallel_1 . \tag{6}$$

$\mathbf{W}$ represents a diagonal matrix with empirical weights, 0.25 or 1 for the presence or absence of motion in each PE line, $\mathbf{A} = \mathcal{F}$ the forward operator, $\lambda = 2$ the regularisation parameter obtained empirically and $\boldsymbol{\Phi}$ the finite differences operator. Equation 6 can be solved for the optimal x^* with a proximal gradient algorithm [7].

3   Experiments and Results

In Fig. 2 we visually compare simulations of motion-affected images without and with B_0 inhomogeneities with a real motion case. This example demonstrates the relevance of including motion-induced field inhomogeneity changes for generating realistic artefact patterns, i.e. more severe blurring and wave-like artefacts appearing for later echoes.

In the following, we use the simulated data to investigate the minimal level of simulated motion, which can be detected by the line classification network. We train the network using four different datasets which were simulated with vary-ing simulation thresholds d_{min}. Figure 3 compares accuracy, ND and WD rates of these networks' predictions on unseen test data (with the same simulation thresholds as for training). The performance in terms of accuracy, ND and WD rate decreases for training and testing the networks with decreasing simulation thresholds. When changing the simulation threshold from 0.5 mm to 0.25 mm, the accuracy drops from 92.28% to 56.31%, which is mainly driven by an increase of the WD rate from 5.25% to 41.02%. This indicates that the network is not able to correctly classify motion-affected PE lines when motion is simulated for time points with less than 0.5 mm average displacement of a 64 mm sphere.

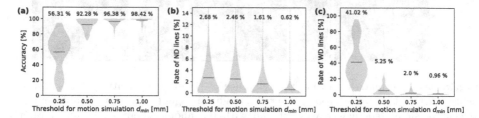

Fig. 3. (a) Test accuracy, (b) rates of non-detected (ND) and (c) wrongly-detected (WD) k-space lines for varying thresholds of simulated motion in train and test data. Mean values are visualised by horizontal lines and given in numbers. All metrics show a decreasing classification performance with decreasing simulation thresholds.

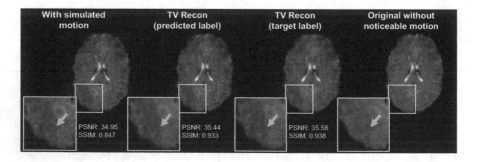

Fig. 4. Demonstration of weighted reconstructions for simulated data. From left to right: images with simulated motion (same data as in Fig. 2, simulation threshold: 0.5 mm), TV reconstructions weighted with predicted labels by the network as well as target labels, and original images. Peak signal-to-noise ratio (PSNR) and structural similarity index (SSIM) [23] with respect to the original images are given below the images. Green arrows indicate an area with subtly reduced artefacts in the weighted reconstructions. (Color figure online)

As an outlook, Fig. 4 demonstrates that the predicted line-wise classifica-tion labels can be used for correcting motion-corrupted images by including the classifications as weights in the DC term of the reconstruction model (Eq. 6).

Visual inspection reveals a subtle decrease of motion artefacts in the weighted reconstruction with target labels and to a certain extent also in the reconstruction with predicted labels. This is in agreement with an improvement of quantitative metrics for both scenarios. However, the weighted reconstructions appear slightly over-smooth compared to the original image.

4   Discussion

We have proposed a physics-aware method to realistically simulate motion artefacts for T_2*-weighted brain MRI in the presence of magnetic field inhomogeneities, which enables supervised training of MoCo models, and, thus, avoids the expensive acquisition of paired in-vivo data. We demonstrated the use of such simulated data for training a k-space line detection network and showed a usecase of this approach for a motion-corrected reconstruction.

Most learning-based MoCo approaches rely on simplistic motion simulation for supervised model training. Oksuz et al. [18], for instance, simulate motion in dynamic cardiac MRI as mistriggering artefacts by exchanging k-space lines between different time points, which does not cover the full range of possible motion artefacts. Others use the MR forward model (Eq. 1) as basis for a more realistic simulation, but only merge a few, discrete motion states and, thus, ignore the continuous nature of real subject motion [3,11,20,24]; or only simulate in-plane motion instead of realistic 3D motion [3,20]. To improve the performance of the developed algorithms on real motion data, the training data generation needs to be as realistic as possible. Thus, our proposed simulation is based on real recorded 3D subject head motion extracted from fMRI time series. Furthermore, due to the sensitivity of T2*-weighted GRE to magnetic field inhomogeneities, our physics-aware simulation incorporates B_0 inhomogeneity changes as secondary motion effects in addition to rigid-body transformations.

The comparison of simulation examples with a real motion case in Fig. 2 demonstrated that the proposed inclusion of B_0 changes in the simulation results in more plausible artefact patterns. Note that - due to inherently long acquisition times - the resolution of quantitative MRI (with typical voxel sizes of 2–3 mm) is commonly lower than for qualitative structural MRI (e.g. T1-weighted MPRAGE scans with voxel sizes < 1 mm). Furthermore, the shown motion artefacts, which mainly manifest in blurring and wave-like patterns, might not appear as severe as in previous studies, where authors simulated motion considerably larger than a voxel size [8,11,14]. However, MoCo is required even for more cooperative subjects in the context of T_2* quantification based on multi-echo GRE data. That is because motion and associated B_0 changes disturb the signal decay over several echo times, even for displacements smaller than the voxel size of 2 mm [5].

To showcase the use of the proposed simulation, we trained a convolutional neural network to detect the presence or absence of motion for every k-space line. First, we have investigated the extent of motion that can be detected by the network. For this, we have varied the simulation threshold for both training and test data. The network was able to classify displacements down to 0.5 mm, corresponding to one quarter of the voxel size, with an accuracy of 92.3%. For smaller simulation thresholds, we have observed a clear performance drop. Considering that the underlying motion curves were extracted from real fMRI time series, a certain degree of noise due to the co-registration can be expected for very small displacements. Thus, using such motion information in the simulation might lead to an overestimation of motion artefacts, which justifies to simulate motion only for time points with displacements larger than 0.5 mm.

As proof-of-principle, we have included the classification labels as weights in the DC term of an iterative reconstruction and demonstrated how the detected motion information can be used for MoCo. The results showed subtly reduced motion artefacts, both visually and quantitatively. However, the reconstructions appeared slightly over-smoothed compared to the original image, which is a common problem when using TV regularisation. In future work we plan to combine line-wise classifications as DC weights with e.g. learning an unrolled optimisation scheme [21]. We further plan to utilise multi-coil raw k-space data to exploit redundancies between coils for improved reconstruction performance.

One limitation of the proposed motion simulation procedure is that we generated random B_0 inhomogeneity variations for each position. More authentic, pose-dependent B_0 inhomogeneity maps can be synthesized by interpolating between B_0 fields of the same subject acquired in different positions [2]. This requires repeated measurements of each subject in different positions, though, which is not feasible for generating large-scale training datasets. Finally, an evaluation of the trained network using real motion corrupted data remains for future work. We just received ethics approval to perform paired in-vivo experiments, which will allow for more thorough quantitative evaluations.

5   Conclusion

We have presented a method for realistic, physics-based motion simulation in T2*-weighted GRE MRI. Our proposed method uses motion curves extracted from real, time-resolved fMRI data and includes motion induced changes in B_0 inhomogeneities. We demonstrated the utility of these simulations for training a line-wise classification network and have been able to detect displacements down to 0.5 mm (a quarter of a voxel). Finally, we outlined how the simulation-based motion detection might be included in the data consistency term of an iterative reconstruction procedure, providing a promising research direction for future work.

Acknowledgements. V.S. and H.E. are partially supported by the Helmholtz Association under the joint research school "Munich School for Data Science - MUDS".

References

1. Retrospective correction of motion in MR images. In: van der Kouwe, A.J., Andre, J.B. (eds.) Motion Correction in MR, vol. 6, pp. 259–267. Academic Press (2022)
2. Brackenier, Y., et al.: Data-driven motion-corrected brain MRI incorporating pose-dependent B0 fields. Magn. Reson. Med. **88**(2), 817–831 (2022)
3. Chatterjee, S., Sciarra, A., Dünnwald, M., Oeltze-Jafra, S., Nürnberger, A., Speck, O.: Retrospective motion correction of MR images using prior-assisted deep learning. In: Proceedings of the 34th Conference on NeurIPS (2020)
4. Cootes, T.F., Taylor, C.J., Cooper, D.H., Graham, J.: Active shape models - their training and application. Comput. Vis. Image Underst. **61**(1), 38–59 (1995)
5. Eichhorn, H., Hammernik, K., Epp, S.M., Karampinos, D.C., Schnabel, J.A., Preibisch, C.: Investigating the impact of motion and associated B0 changes on oxygenation sensitive MRI through realistic simulations. In: Proceedings of the International Society for Magnetic Resonance in Medicine, vol. 31 (2023)
6. Gersing, A.S., et al.: Mapping of cerebral metabolic rate of oxygen using dynamic susceptibility contrast and blood oxygen level dependent MR imaging in acute ischemic stroke. Neuroradiology **57**, 1253–1261 (2015)
7. Hammernik, K., Knoll, F.: Machine learning for image reconstruction. In: Zhou, S.K., Rueckert, D., Fichtinger, G. (eds.) Handbook of Medical Image Computing and Computer Assisted Intervention, pp. 25–64. Academic Press (2020)
8. Haskell, M.W., et al.: Network accelerated motion estimation and reduction (NAMER): convolutional neural network guided retrospective motion correction using a separable motion model. Magn. Reson. Med. **82**(4), 1452–1461 (2019)
9. Hirsch, N.M., Toth, V., Förschler, A., Kooijman, H., Zimmer, C., Preibisch, C.: Technical considerations on the validity of blood oxygenation level-dependent-based MR assessment of vascular deoxygenation: Bold-based assessment of vascular deoxygenation. NMR Biomed. **27**(7), 853–862 (2014)
10. Jiang, W., et al.: Motion robust high resolution 3D free-breathing pulmonary MRI using dynamic 3D image self-navigator. Magn. Reson. Med. **79**(6), 2954–2967 (2018)
11. Johnson, P.M., Drangova, M.: Conditional generative adversarial network for 3D rigid-body motion correction in MRI. Magn. Reson. Med. **82**(3), 901–910 (2019)
12. Kaczmarz, S., et al.: Hemodynamic impairments within individual watershed areas in asymptomatic carotid artery stenosis by multimodal MRI. J. Cerebral Blood Flow Metaboli. **41**(2), 380–396 (2021)
13. Kingma, D.P., Ba, J.: Adam: a method for stochastic optimization. In: Proceedings of the 3rd ICLR (2015)
14. Küstner, T., Armanious, K., Yang, J., Yang, B., Schick, F., Gatidis, S.: Retrospective correction of motion-affected MR images using deep learning frameworks. Magn. Reson. Med. **82**(4), 1527–1540 (2019)
15. Liu, J., de Zwart, J.A., van Gelderen, P., Murphy-Boesch, J., Duyn, J.H.: Effect of head motion on MRI B0 field distribution. Magn. Reson. Med. **80**(6), 2538–2548 (2018)
16. Magerkurth, J., et al.: Quantitative T2* -mapping based on multi-slice multiple gradient echo flash imaging: retrospective correction for subject motion effects: Movement correction in T2* mapping. Magn. Reson. Med. **66**(4), 989–997 (2011)
17. Nöth, U., Volz, S., Hattingen, E., Deichmann, R.: An improved method for retrospective motion correction in quantitative T2* mapping. Neuroimage **92**, 106–119 (2014)

18. Oksuz, I., et al.: Deep learning-based detection and correction of cardiac MR motion artefacts during reconstruction for high-quality segmentation. IEEE Trans. Med. Imaging **39**(12), 4001–4010 (2020)
19. Preibisch, C., et al.: Characterizing hypoxia in human glioma: a simultaneous multimodal MRI and PET study. NMR Biomed. **30**(11), e3775 (2017)
20. Rotman, M., Brada, R., Beniaminy, I., Ahn, S., Hardy, C.J., Wolf, L.: Correcting motion artifacts in MRI scans using a deep neural network with automatic motion timing detection. In: Medical Imaging 2021: Physics of Medical Imaging, vol. 11595, pp. 296–305. SPIE (2021)
21. Schlemper, J., Caballero, J., Hajnal, J.V., Price, A.N., Rueckert, D.: A deep cascade of convolutional neural networks for dynamic MR image reconstruction. IEEE Trans. Med. Imaging **37**(2), 491–503 (2018)
22. Spieker, V., et al.: Deep learning for retrospective motion correction in MRI: a comprehensive review, arXiv: 2305.06739
23. Wang, Z., Bovik, A., Sheikh, H., Simoncelli, E.: Image quality assessment: from error visibility to structural similarity. IEEE Trans. Image Process. **13**(4), 600–612 (2004)
24. Xu, X., et al.: Learning-based motion artifact removal networks for quantitative R2∗ mapping. Mag. Res. Med. **88**(1), 106–119 (2022)

Unsupervised Heteromodal Physics-Informed Representation of MRI Data: Tackling Data Harmonisation, Imputation and Domain Shift

Pedro Borges[1(✉)], Virginia Fernandez[1], Petru Daniel Tudosiu[1],
Parashkev Nachev[2], Sebastien Ourselin[1], and M. Jorge Cardoso[1]

[1] School of Biomedical Engineering and Imaging Sciences, KCL, London, UK
`pedro.borges@kcl.ac.uk`
[2] Queen Square Institute of Neurology, UCL, London, UK

Abstract. Clinical MR imaging is typically qualitative, i.e. the observed signal reflects the underlying tissue contrast, but the measurements are not meaningful when taken in isolation. Quantitative MR imaging maps are rarely acquired due to time and complexity constraints but directly measure intrinsic tissue properties, allowing for explicit tissue characterisation and MR contrast simulation. A machine learning network trained on quantitative MRI would circumvent the need to design contrast-agnostic models, minimise domain shift issues, and reduce complex data pre-processing. Such models would also be future-proof by design, anticipating new qualitative sequence developments and changes in acquisition parameters. In this work, we propose a new Bloch-equation-based physics-informed unsupervised network that learns to map qualitative MR data to their quantitative equivalents without the need for paired qualitative-quantitative data. Furthermore, we make the proposed model robust to missing data, enabling us to map any arbitrary set of qualitative data from a patient into quantitative Multi-Parametric Maps (MPMs). We demonstrate that the estimated MPMs are a robust and invariant data representation, are self-consistent, enable missing data imputation, and facilitate data harmonisation from multiple sites while bridging algorithmic domain gaps.

1 Introduction

Magnetic Resonance Imaging (MRI) is widely employed to identify and monitor a wide range of pathologies and to probe neurological function [2,4,14]. In practice, MR data is typically qualitative, tailored to optimise contrast for a specific task [11] but insufficient to compute the underlying tissue properties that determine the image intensity, namely the longitudinal relaxation time, T_1, the transverse relaxation time, T_2, and the proton density PD. MPMs describing

---

Supplementary Information The online version contains supplementary material available at https://doi.org/10.1007/978-3-031-44689-4_6.

J. M. Wolterink et al. (Eds.): SASHIMI 2023, LNCS 14288, pp. 53–63, 2023.
https://doi.org/10.1007/978-3-031-44689-4_6

these properties allow for such useful applications as *contrast simulation* [20], or disease characterisation [3,5], but acquiring them requires multiple multi-echo scanning sessions, which is often too time-consuming to be practical.

Various methods seek to derive MPMs from more easily acquired images, such as single multi-echo sequences [9], MR fingerprinting (MRF) [12,15], or even single qualitative images regressed by parameter estimation and CLONE models [18].

Promisingly, Dalca et al. [25] avoid the need for MPMs for training by generating all three MPMs using an unsupervised physics-forward model.

The primary issue with the above-cited works is that they rely on data acquired under particular conditions and thus cannot leverage the heterogeneity/wealth of real medical data to validate their work. While their aim is, for the most part, to facilitate the MRF process, we underscore the need for a qualitative-to-quantitative translation method that can be trained and applied to typical MR datasets, which can boast a variety (or scarcity) of MR sequences per subject. At first glance, it seems like this is an intractable task, as for every qualitative voxel, three separate quantitative valued voxels need to be predicted. However, as values in MPMs are strongly correlated via the underlying anatomy, the task's ill-posedness is reduced.

Based on this premise, we propose an unsupervised, multi-modal, attention-based method with a physics-based forward model to convert multi-/single-modal data into their quantitative T_1, T_2, and PD equivalents. Our approach prioritizes flexibility and the ability to create an invariant representation for a subject regardless of available modalities. Unlike previous works, our model can accommodate heterogeneous, modality-scarce data. We demonstrate its efficacy through reconstruction consistency and missing modality imputation, with a final examination of the effectiveness of our imputed data on a downstream segmentation task.

2   Methods

2.1   Modelling the MR Signal via Static Equations

The signal in qualitative MRI depends on the properties of the underlying tissues. These underlying properties can be probed and highlighted by carefully selecting sequences and sequence parameters to suit the task. Given the underlying tissue properties, an MR simulator can generate images according to the chosen sequence and sequence parameters. At the most straightforward end of the spectrum, static equations offer an approximation of the signal given the sequence parameters and underlying MR properties of the examined tissues. These equations are derived analytically by considering the magnetisation value immediately before read-out, thus relinquishing the need for temporal considerations. This makes them perfectly suited for the task at hand, as their computational demands are low, allowing them to slot in seamlessly into a live deep-learning setting, as seen in such works as [6,18,25]. We present the static equation formulations for the three sequences that we choose to generate quantitative maps from, namely those for MPRAGE [13], FLAIR [16], and spin echo (SE) [16], respectively, for the signal at a single voxel at location x:

$$b_{\text{MPRAGE}}(x) = G \cdot PD(x)\left(1 - \frac{2e^{\frac{-TI}{T_1(x)}}}{1 + e^{\frac{-TR}{T_1(x)}}}\right), \tag{1}$$

$$b_{\text{FLAIR}}(x) = G \cdot PD(x)\left(1 - 2e^{\frac{-TI}{T1(x)}} + e^{\frac{-TI}{T1(x)}}\right)e^{\frac{-TE}{T2(x)}}, \tag{2}$$

$$b_{\text{SE}}(x) = G \cdot PD(x)\left(1 - e^{\frac{-TI}{T1(x)}}\right)e^{\frac{-TE}{T2(x)}}, \tag{3}$$

Note that T_1, T_2, and PD are all a function of space, x. TR represents repetition time, TI inversion time, and TE echo time. G is a dimensionless parameter that models the scanner gain and alters only the global intensity.

We employ these sets of equations for reconstructing images from generated qualitative maps to ascertain consistency to the input and derive the main loss that drives the learning process.

2.2 Models

One could frame this MPM regression as an inverse problem that does not require the presence of a neural network in a manner similar to that described in [24]. However, such methods could not account for missing modalities and spatial interactions between signals, and works have shown that neural networks outcompete prior methods for image reconstruction [27], so it follows that neural networks are poised as the best candidates for solving this problem.

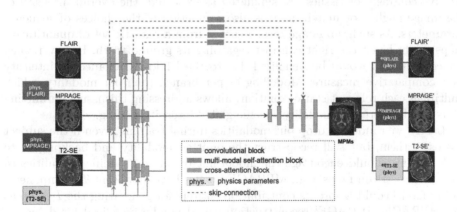

Fig. 1. Proposed pipeline: Intra-subject modalities are fed through modality-specific encoders, incorporating cross-attention with the respective sequence parameters. Multi-modality self-attention convolutions are performed on the modality-aggregated encoded features and passed via skip connections to the decoder. The model outputs quantitative T_1, T_2, and PD maps, which can then be passed through physics models to generate images.

The training pipeline is described in Fig. 1. The individual modality encoder branches and the decoder branch follow U-Net's structure. Different modal images will exhibit more pertinent features for reconstructing specific quantitative map components than others. Therefore, we want to leverage shared information throughout the modality branches to generate quantitative maps of the highest fidelity. To this end, we leverage the Multi-Modality Self-Attention Aware (MMSA) convolution proposed by [17]. This convolution can adaptively modulate how much each modality contributes to different output components. We employ the MMSA across our three modality branches on the feature maps following each of the four downsampling steps in the multi-path encoder. Similarly to each single-modality encoder, we adopt a U-Net-like structure for our decoder. This structure comprises three upsampling blocks: a "3D convolution + leaky-relu + 3D upsampling", a "3D convolution + leaky-relu" and a final "3D convolution + Softplus". The Softplus activation ensures that the output is always greater than or equal to zero, as tissue parameters cannot be negative.

Ultimately, we want the output to represent the quantitative maps for T_1, T_2, and PD. We enforce this by passing the decoder output through our physics forward model (represented by Eq. 1 - 3) in conjunction with the relevant physics parameters to reconstruct a modality. We impose an L1 loss between the physics reconstruction and the input modality, as a good modality reconstruction is contingent on generating realistic quantitative MPM maps — this allows us to train the models with arbitrary qualitative data and without paired MPMs. We also include a perceptual loss [26] to enhance the finer details.

Crucially, a missing component hampers our ability to precisely perform the core reconstructions for training our models, namely the scalar gain parameter, which, recall, features in all our static equations as G. In its absence, while the relative contrasts of tissues are simulated as expected, the overall intensity of the image might not match, as it is also a function of the choices of sequence parameters. As such, an image reconstructed from a realistic set of quantitative maps might boast the right contrast regarding its ground truth. However, such a reconstruction would be penalised due to the L1 loss's reliance on intensity as a comparative measure. Modelling G per branch (one per modality, which multiplies each relevant static equation) allows addressing this issue, permitting post-MPM generation modality-specific global intensity scaling.

Lastly, we randomly drop out modalities during training, even if the subject possesses them, but still reconstruct the omitted modality and backpropagate its loss. This should encourage the model not to rely on specific modalities to reconstruct certain maps. e.g., MPRAGE images have an absent T_2 component, so the model could ignore its contribution entirely for generating the T_2 map as the MPRAGE-MPRAGE' reconstruction would not be penalised for doing so. However, if the subject has a T2-SE image that has not been passed as input but must still be reconstructed, then the model can no longer resort to such tactics.

2.3 Pre-processing and Data

We have employed images from the UK Biobank (UKB) [22], SABRE [23], and OASIS-3 [19] to train and validate our models. Regarding relevant modality variety, we leverage UKB's FLAIR and MPRAGE images, while for SABRE, we use MPRAGE, FLAIR, and T2-SE. Only some subjects in either dataset contain all relevant modalities, but since our pipeline is designed to account for such cases, we included them. To this end, we used 40,567 UKB participants and 932 SABRE participants, with an 80/10/10 train/val/test % split. Due to the data imbalance, we operate under a stratified training scheme. For every epoch, the network sees all the PD-1 training data and an equally-sized chunk of Biobank training data. Subsequent epochs will see the same PD-1 data but a separate, equally-sized chunk of Biobank training data. This ensures that T2-SE images are adequately represented at every epoch.

For the training of our segmentation network, 160 MPRAGE images from GENFI [21] were used. UniRes [7,8] was employed to register all images to a 1mm isotropic MNI space, then cropped to $160 \times 224 \times 160$ to exclude non-cranial regions.

3 Experiments and Results

3.1 Consistency

As covered in the introduction, there is no task-equivalent baseline to the presented method, as existing MPM-reconstruction techniques rely either on multi-echo data or assume the existence of MPM datasets (we explicitly avoid both to replicate typical clinical data). Thus our analyses focus on internal consistency and imputation, as well as validation on a downstream segmentation task.

We denote consistency as the reconstruction fidelity of modalities to which the model has been made privy, e.g., if an MPRAGE and FLAIR image is passed as input, are the generated quantitative tissue maps faithful enough to reconstruct realistically said modalities, when passed through the respective static equations? Consistency is assessed by considering all modality combinations that feature the modality whose consistency is being analysed.

Table 1 showcases the MSE and MS-SSIM for this experiment (UKB does not contain any T2-SE images; therefore, those cells involving the presence of T2-SE and this dataset are left blank). Figure 2 shows regenerated FLAIRs for a subject resulting from varying input modalities alongside its real counterpart. All metrics indicate consistent results, though it is interesting to note certain drops in performance when increasing the number of input modalities; Fig. 2 showcases the phenomenon perfectly. While the regeneration that arises from solely having a FLAIR as input is the most precise, the addition of both T2-SE and MPRAGE has sharpened the details in the image. The same phenomenon can be seen for FLAIR-reconstructed images for OASIS-3, the reconstructions that feature MPRAGE images exhibit significantly lower scores than their non-MPRAGE counterparts. We verified qualitatively that the through-plane details of the FLAIR (which had slice thicknesses of 5mm originally and lacked detail even when super-resolved) too were significantly enhanced by MPRAGE's inclusion, which again explains the drop in MS-SSIM score.

Table 1. Mean MSE and MS-SSIM for the consistency experiment, shown for all possible combinations of MRI modalities, including at least the reconstructed modality. ●: Modality present, ○: Modality absent. MSE have been multiplied by 10^3. Bold values represent statistically best performances.

Regenerated modality	Input modalities			UKB		SABRE		OASIS-3	
	FLAIR	MPRAGE	T2-SE	MSE	MS-SSIM	MSE	MS-SSIM	MSE	MS-SSIM
FLAIR	●	○	○	$0.36_{0.11}$	$\mathbf{0.9991_{0.0002}}$	$\mathbf{0.29_{0.13}}$	$\mathbf{0.9971_{0.0009}}$	$\mathbf{15.68_{30.61}}$	$\mathbf{0.8805_{0.1077}}$
	●	●	○	$\mathbf{0.34_{0.10}}$	$0.9988_{0.0003}$	$1.09_{0.17}$	$0.9906_{0.0009}$	$33.14_{31.50}$	$0.6454_{0.0876}$
	●	○	●	-	-	$2.91_{0.79}$	$0.9598_{0.0145}$	$48.05_{8.52}$	$0.7509_{0.0543}$
	●	●	●	-	-	$3.48_{0.32}$	$0.9506_{0.0051}$	$53.66_{28.65}$	$0.5742_{0.0743}$
MPRAGE	○	●	○	$0.19_{0.16}$	$0.9975_{0.0027}$	$\mathbf{1.51_{0.40}}$	$\mathbf{0.9927_{0.0009}}$	$13.59_{5.00}$	$0.8817_{0.0124}$
	●	●	○	$\mathbf{0.06_{0.02}}$	$\mathbf{0.9992_{0.0003}}$	$1.59_{0.38}$	$0.9926_{0.0011}$	$\mathbf{5.60_{1.47}}$	$\mathbf{0.9219_{0.0216}}$
	○	●	●	-	-	$1.95_{0.44}$	$0.9880_{0.0016}$	$28.81_{12.75}$	$0.8580_{0.0331}$
	●	●	●	-	-	$2.14_{0.50}$	$0.9869_{0.0025}$	$5.88_{0.77}$	$0.8914_{0.0268}$
T2-SE	○	○	●	-	-	$\mathbf{0.48_{0.15}}$	$\mathbf{0.9968_{0.0007}}$	$36.96_{19.37}$	$\mathbf{0.8047_{0.0739}}$
	●	○	●	-	-	$5.39_{2.06}$	$0.9200_{0.0343}$	$53.52_{11.36}$	$0.7558_{0.0252}$
	○	●	●	-	-	$8.67_{1.28}$	$0.8876_{0.0184}$	$58.81_{16.75}$	$0.7280_{0.0431}$
	●	●	●	-	-	$1.18_{1.64}$	$0.8532_{0.0261}$	$59.29_{13.64}$	$0.7072_{0.0273}$

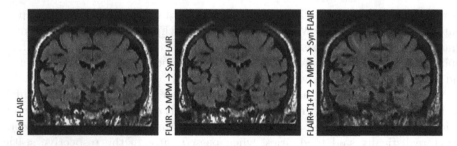

Fig. 2. Consistency visualisation: Real FLAIR (Left), regenerated FLAIR from the predicted MPMs given a real FLAIR (Middle), regenerated FLAIR from the predicted MPMs given a real FLAIR, MPRAGE, T2-SE (Right).

3.2 Imputation

We denote imputation as the reconstruction fidelity of modalities to which the model has not been made privy, e.g., if a FLAIR and T2-SE are passed as input, how accurate is the MPRAGE image that is simulated from the generated quantitative maps? As with the consistency experiment, we consider all modality combinations that do not feature the modality whose consistency is being assessed when carrying out this analysis.

Table 2 and Fig. 3 showcase imputation results. The UKB dataset T2-SE's caveat holds as before; accordingly, such results are not applicable. For UKB, the imputation results are excellent; clearly, there is a significant amount of overlapping information in these modality pairs for this dataset. To a lesser extent, the same can be said of the FLAIR-MPRAGE permutations for SABRE. Imputations involving T2-SE incur the greatest drop in performance. We observed that the CSF reconstruction was lacking, which could partly be explained by the lack of variety in the way this tissue presents in both FLAIR and MPRAGE images, but general tissue contrast expectations were still met.

Table 2. Mean MSE and MS-SSIM for the imputation experiment, for all possible combinations of MRI modalities that do not include the modality being reconstructed. •: Modality present, o: Modality absent. MSE have been multiplied by 10^3. Bold values represent statistically best performances.

Regenerated modality	Input modalities			UKB		SABRE	
	FLAIR	MPRAGE	T2-SE	MSE	MS-SSIM	MSE	MS-SSIM
FLAIR	o	•	o	**8.73**$_{5.84}$	**0.8840**$_{0.0538}$	10.84$_{1.56}$	0.8281$_{0.0164}$
	o	o	•	-	-	41.20$_{12.70}$	0.5262$_{0.1613}$
	o	•	•	-	-	13.18$_{1.25}$	0.7659$_{0.0258}$
MPRAGE	•	o	o	**4.97**$_{0.91}$	**0.9244**$_{0.0149}$	11.83$_{1.45}$	0.8849$_{0.0135}$
	o	o	•	-	-	27.40$_{3.91}$	0.5862$_{0.0527}$
	•	o	•	-	-	13.47$_{2.04}$	0.8346$_{0.0151}$
T2-SE	•	o	o	-	-	31.19$_{9.11}$	0.5984$_{0.1255}$
	o	•	o	-	-	31.35$_{2.71}$	0.4782$_{0.0496}$
	•	•	o	-	-	34.79$_{3.43}$	0.5363$_{0.0427}$

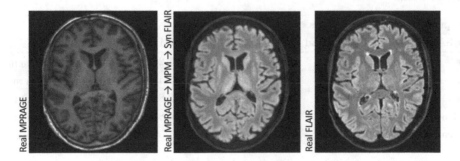

Fig. 3. Imputation visualisation: Input real MPRAGE (Left), regenerated FLAIR from real MPRAGE (Middle), and real FLAIR (Right)

3.3 Segmentation with Imputed Data

In the absence of a particular modality for a given dataset, can we use our model to impute the missing modality using those available in the context of a downstream task? We test this in the context of multi-tissue brain segmentation. For this, we source 160 MPRAGE images from GENFI to train our segmentation network. From SABRE we select 100 subjects from the inference set, each with a FLAIR, T2-SE, and MPRAGE image. We task our model with generating quantitative maps from only the former two modalities (thus simulating an MPRAGE-absent scenario), fed through the MPRAGE static equation to generate corresponding MPRAGE images. Figure 4 showcases an MPRAGE regenerated from a FLAIR and T2-SE alongside its real MPRAGE counterpart.

The segmentation model is trained using the standard optimised U-Net sourced from the MONAI framework [1], over five folds, with a 120/ 20/ 20 train/val/test split. Ground truth labels for both datasets are obtained using GIF [10].

The results are shown in Table 3. We validate the segmentation model on regenerated MPRAGEs generated using all three combinations of FLAIR and T2-SE, and on the real SABRE FLAIR images. The latter grants us a baseline in absentia: what performance could you expect if you had no choice but to validate the model on the available modalities? Finally, we evaluate the model on the true MPRAGEs of SABRE. We carry out signed-rank Wilcoxon tests to ascertain that the results the model validated on regenerated MPRAGEs always (barring CSF) outperform validations performed on real FLAIRs, regardless of the starting input combinations. However, there is still a statistically significant performance deficit when compared to real data, which is not unexpected, as previous results have shown how imputation is a harder task than consistency.

Table 3. Segmentation imputation experiment, featuring Dice scores for MPRAGE images regenerated from all possible combinations of MRI modalities, absent MPRAGE; Dice scores on the real FLAIRs; and Dice scores on the real MPRAGEs, for six classes.

Input modalities		Dice scores					
FLAIR	T2-SE	Background	CSF	DGM	GM	Brainstem	WM
●	○	$98.31_{0.67}$	$49.18_{11.75}$	$59.17_{9.63}$	$61.26_{7.32}$	$63.56_{13.26}$	$61.30_{10.10}$
○	●	$97.65_{0.50}$	$42.03_{7.60}$	$54.88_{9.69}$	$45.47_{3.22}$	$71.39_{11.93}$	$63.25_{4.70}$
●	●	$98.19_{0.67}$	$39.79_{9.30}$	$55.48_{11.10}$	$62.89_{9.76}$	$66.05_{17.64}$	$67.09_{10.10}$
Real FLAIRs		$95.77_{3.04}$	$47.60_{16.33}$	$42.85_{18.00}$	$34.82_{11.40}$	$47.08_{26.70}$	$42.11_{10.48}$
Real MPRAGEs		$97.20_{1.69}$	$70.73_{9.25}$	$65.70_{18.04}$	$71.56_{11.44}$	$65.52_{17.74}$	$78.13_{9.95}$

Inputs		MPMs			Gen.	Real
FLAIR	T2-SE	T1	T2	PD	MPRAGE	MPRAGE

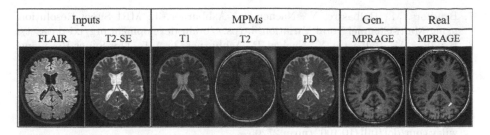

Fig. 4. Example MPRAGE imputation for segmentation experiment using subject FLAIR and T2-SE, with intermediary MPM shown.

4   Discussion and Conclusion

This work showcases an input-modality-flexible, attention-based, physics-informed, unsupervised method for generating quantitative MR tissue maps from a gamut of starting image combinations, be they scarce or plentiful. We thoroughly validate our model via regeneration and imputation analyses and via a downstream segmentation task. This work paves the way for translating typical data into an invariant space, dispensing with the need to train dataset-specific models.

There is an irreducible error in estimating tissue parameters in the absence of sufficient tissue contrast of the image or images available as input; thus, incorporating uncertainty modelling into our networks would give them an additional level of introspection and safety. Furthermore, including an adversarial component on the generated quantitative maps could mitigate these issues by attaching quality priors based on distilled information from entire datasets, improving the appearance of the quantitative maps, the reconstructed images, or both.

References

1. Project MONAI. DOI: 10.5281/zenodo.4323059
2. Abd-Ellah, M.K., Awad, A.I., Khalaf, A.A.M., Hamed, H.F.A.: A review on brain tumor diagnosis from MRI images: practical implications, key achievements, and lessons learned. Magn. Reson. Imaging **61**, 300–318 (2019). https://doi.org/10.1016/j.mri.2019.05.028
3. Andreasen, N.C., et al.: T1 and T2 relaxation times in schizophrenia as measured with magnetic resonance imaging. Schizophr. Res. **5**(3), 223–232 (1991). https://doi.org/10.1016/0920-9964(91)90080-B
4. Bandettini, P.A.: Twenty years of functional MRI: the science and the stories. Neuroimage **62**(2), 575–588 (2012). https://doi.org/10.1016/j.neuroimage.2012.04.026
5. Baudrexel, S., et al.: Quantitative mapping of T1 and T2* discloses nigral and brainstem pathology in early Parkinson's disease. Neuroimage **51**(2), 512–520 (2010). https://doi.org/10.1016/j.neuroimage.2010.03.005
6. Borges, P., et al.: Physics-informed brain MRI segmentation. 11827 LNCS, 100–109 (2020). https://doi.org/10.1007/978-3-030-32778-1_11

7. Brudfors, M., Balbastre, Y., Nachev, P., Ashburner, J.: MRI Super-Resolution using Multi-Channel Total Variation. https://brain-development.org/ixi-dataset/
8. Brudfors, M., Balbastre, Y., Nachev, P., Ashburner, J.: A Tool for Super-Resolving Multimodal Clinical MRI (2019). 10.48550/arxiv.1909.01140. https://arxiv.org/abs/1909.01140v1
9. Cai, C., et al.: Single-shot T2 mapping using overlapping-echo detachment planar imaging and a deep convolutional neural network. Magn. Reson. Med. **80**(5), 2202–2214 (2018). https://doi.org/10.1002/MRM.27205. https://onlinelibrary.wiley.com/doi/full/10.1002/mrm.27205
10. Cardoso, M.J., et al.: Geodesic information flows: spatially-variant graphs and their application to segmentation and fusion. IEEE Trans. Med. Imaging **34**(9), 1976–1988 (2015)
11. Chavhan, G.B.: Appropriate selection of MRI sequences for common scenarios in clinical practice. Pediatr. Radiol. **46**(6), 740–747 (2016). https://doi.org/10.1007/s00247-016-3556-4
12. Cohen, O., Zhu, B., Rosen, M.S.: MR fingerprinting Deep RecOnstruction NEtwork (DRONE). Magn. Reson. Med. **80**(3), 885–894 (2018). https://doi.org/10.1002/MRM.27198, https://onlinelibrary.wiley.com/doi/full/10.1002/mrm.27198
13. Deichmann, R., Good, C.D., Josephs, O., Ashburner, J., Turner, R.: Optimization of 3-D MP-RAGE sequences for structural brain imaging. NeuroImage **12**(1), 112–127 (2000). https://doi.org/10.1006/NIMG.2000.0601,https://pubmed.ncbi.nlm.nih.gov/10875908/
14. Desikan, R., et al.: Automated MRI measures identify individuals with mild cognitive impairment and Alzheimer's disease. Brain : J. Neurol. **132**(Pt 8), 2048–2057 (2009). https://doi.org/10.1093/BRAIN/AWP123, https://pubmed.ncbi.nlm.nih.gov/19460794/
15. Fang, Z., et al.: Deep learning for fast and spatially constrained tissue quantification from highly accelerated data in magnetic resonance fingerprinting. IEEE Trans. Med. Imaging **38**(10), 2364–2374 (2019). https://doi.org/10.1109/TMI.2019.2899328
16. Hornak, J.: The Basics of MRI. https://www.cis.rit.edu/htbooks/mri/
17. Jia, X., Liu, Y., Yang, Z., Yang, D.: Multi-modality self-attention aware deep network for 3D biomedical segmentation. BMC Medical Informatics and Decision Making **20**(3), 1–7 (jul 2020). https://doi.org/10.1186/s12911-020-1109-0
18. Jog, A., et al.: MR image synthesis by contrast learning on neighborhood ensembles. Med. Image Anal. **24**(1), 63–76 (2015)
19. Marcus, D.S., Wang, T.H., Parker, J., Csernansky, J.G., Morris, J.C., Buckner, R.L.: Open access series of imaging studies (OASIS): cross-sectional MRI data in young, middle aged, nondemented, and demented older adults. J. Cogn. Neurosci. **19**(9), 1498–1507 (2007). https://doi.org/10.1162/JOCN.2007.19.9.1498
20. Protti, A., et al.: Development and validation of a new MRI simulation technique that can reliably estimate optimal in vivo scanning parameters in a glioblastoma murine model. PloS ONE **13**(7) (2018). https://doi.org/10.1371/JOURNAL.PONE.0200611, https://pubmed.ncbi.nlm.nih.gov/30036367/
21. Rohrer, J.D., et al.: Presymptomatic cognitive and neuroanatomical changes in genetic frontotemporal dementia in the Genetic Frontotemporal dementia Initiative (GENFI) study: a cross-sectional analysis. Articles Lancet Neurol. **14**, 253–62 (2015). https://doi.org/10.1016/S1474-4422(14)70324-2, https://dx.doi.org/10.1016/

22. Sudlow, C., et al.: UK Biobank: an open access resource for identifying the causes of a wide range of complex diseases of middle and old age. PLOS Med. **12**(3), e1001779 (2015). https://doi.org/10.1371/JOURNAL.PMED.1001779, https://journals.plos.org/plosmedicine/article?id=10.1371/journal.pmed.1001779
23. Tillin, T., et al.: Southall and Brent Revisited: Cohort profile of SABRE, a UK population-based comparison of cardiovascular disease and diabetes in people of European, Indian Asian and African Caribbean origins. Int. J. epidemiol. **41**(1), 33–42 (2012). https://doi.org/10.1093/IJE/DYQ175, https://pubmed.ncbi.nlm.nih.gov/21044979/
24. Ulyanov, D., Vedaldi, A., Lempitsky, V., Ulyanov, D., Vedaldi, A., Lempitsky, V.: Deep image prior. Int. J. Comput. Vis. **128**(7), 1867–1888 (2017). https://doi.org/10.1007/s11263-020-01303-4, arXiv:1711.10925v4
25. Varadarajan, D., Bouman, K.L., van der Kouwe, A., Fischl, B., Dalca, A.V.: Unsupervised learning of MRI tissue properties using MRI physics models (2021). arXiv.org:2107.02704v1
26. Zhang, R., Isola, P., Efros, A.A., Shechtman, E., Wang, O.: The unreasonable effectiveness of deep features as a perceptual metric. In: 2018 IEEE/CVF Conference on Computer Vision and Pattern Recognition (CVPR), pp. 586–595 (2018). https://doi.org/10.1109/CVPR.2018.00068
27. Zhu, B., Liu, J.Z., Cauley, S.F., Rosen, B.R., Rosen, M.S.: Image reconstruction by domain-transform manifold learning. Nature 2018 555:7697 555(7697), 487–492 (2018). https://doi.org/10.1038/nature25988, https://www.nature.com/articles/nature25988

TAI-GAN: Temporally and Anatomically Informed GAN for Early-to-Late Frame Conversion in Dynamic Cardiac PET Motion Correction

Xueqi Guo[1]([✉])[iD], Luyao Shi[2][iD], Xiongchao Chen[1][iD], Bo Zhou[1][iD],
Qiong Liu[1][iD], Huidong Xie[1][iD], Yi-Hwa Liu[1], Richard Palyo[3],
Edward J. Miller[1][iD], Albert J. Sinusas[1][iD], Bruce Spottiswoode[4], Chi Liu[1],
and Nicha C. Dvornek[1][iD]

[1] Yale University, New Haven, CT 06511, USA
{xueqi.guo,chi.liu,nicha.dvornek}@yale.edu
[2] IBM Research, San Jose, CA 95120, USA
[3] Yale New Haven Hospital, New Haven, CT 06511, USA
[4] Siemens Medical Solutions USA, Inc., Knoxville, TN 37932, USA

Abstract. The rapid tracer kinetics of rubidium-82 (^{82}Rb) and high variation of cross-frame distribution in dynamic cardiac positron emission tomography (PET) raise significant challenges for inter-frame motion correction, particularly for the early frames where conventional intensity-based image registration techniques are not applicable. Alternatively, a promising approach utilizes generative methods to handle the tracer distribution changes to assist existing registration methods. To improve frame-wise registration and parametric quantification, we propose a Temporally and Anatomically Informed Generative Adversarial Network (TAI-GAN) to transform the early frames into the late reference frame using an all-to-one mapping. Specifically, a feature-wise linear modulation layer encodes channel-wise parameters generated from temporal tracer kinetics information, and rough cardiac segmentations with local shifts serve as the anatomical information. We validated our proposed method on a clinical ^{82}Rb PET dataset and found that our TAI-GAN can produce converted early frames with high image quality, comparable to the real reference frames. After TAI-GAN conversion, motion estimation accuracy and clinical myocardial blood flow (MBF) quantification were improved compared to using the original frames. Our code is published at https://github.com/gxq1998/TAI-GAN.

Keywords: frame conversion · cardiac PET · motion correction

1 Introduction

Compared to other non-invasive imaging techniques, dynamic cardiac positron emission tomography (PET) myocardial perfusion imaging increases the accu-

Supplementary Information The online version contains supplementary material available at https://doi.org/10.1007/978-3-031-44689-4_7.

racy of coronary artery disease detection [20]. After tracer injection, a dynamic frame sequence is acquired over several minutes until the myocardium is well perfused. The time-activity curves (TACs) are collected in the myocardium tissue and left ventricle blood pool (LVBP) using regions of interest (ROIs) derived from the reconstructed frames. The myocardial blood flow (MBF) is then quantified through kinetic modeling using myocardium and LVBP TACs.

However, the inter-frame motion will cause spatial misalignment across the dynamic frames, resulting in incorrect TAC measurements and a major impact on both ROI-based and voxel-based MBF quantification [12]. The high variation of cross-frame distribution originating from the rapid tracer kinetics of rubidium-82 (^{82}Rb) further complicates inter-frame motion correction, especially for the early frames when the injected tracer is concentrated in the blood pool and has not been well distributed in the myocardium. Most existing motion correction studies and clinical software focus solely on the later frames in the myocardial perfusion phase [3,16,26]. Although deep learning-based dynamic PET motion correction has outperformed conventional techniques [9,10,27], few focused on ^{82}Rb cardiac PET. An automatic motion correction network was proposed for ^{82}Rb cardiac PET under supervised learning using simulated translational motion [22], but the method requires training two separate models to handle the discrepancy between early and late frames, which is inconvenient and computationally expensive.

Alternatively, the usage of image synthesis and modality conversion has been proposed to improve optimization in multi-modality image registration [4,15,18], mostly involving magnetic resonance imaging. In FDG dynamic PET, converting early frames to the corresponding late frame using a generative adversarial network (GAN) is a promising way to overcome the barrier of tracer differences and aid motion correction [24,25]. However, this recent method trains one-to-one mappings for each specific early frame, which is impractical to implement and also difficult to generalize to new acquisitions. Moreover, the tracer kinetics and related temporal analysis are not incorporated in model training, which might be a challenge when directly applied to ^{82}Rb cardiac PET.

In this work, we propose a Temporally and Anatomically Informed GAN (TAI-GAN) as an all-to-one mapping to convert all the early frames into the last reference frame. A feature-wise linear modulation (FiLM) layer encodes channel-wise parameters generated from the blood pool TACs and the temporal frame index, providing additional temporal information to the generator. The rough segmentations of the right ventricle blood pool (RVBP), LVBP, and myocardium with local shifts serve as the auxiliary anatomical information. Most current work applying GAN+FiLM models encode text or semantic information for natural images [1,2,17] and metadata for medical images [6,21], while we innovatively propose encoding dynamic PET tracer distribution changes. TAI-GAN is the first work incorporating both temporal and anatomical information into the GAN for dynamic cardiac PET frame conversion, with the ability to handle high tracer distribution variability and prevent spatial mismatch.

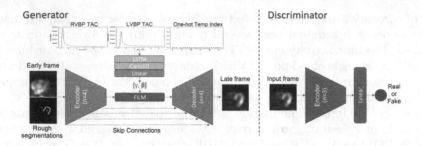

Fig. 1. The structure of the proposed early-to-late frame conversion network TAI-GAN.

2   Methods

2.1   Dataset

This study includes 85 clinical ^{82}Rb PET scans (55 rest and 30 regadenoson-induced stress) that were acquired from 59 patients at the Yale New Haven Hospital using a GE Discovery 690 PET/CT scanner and defined by the clinical team to be nearly motion-free, with Yale Institutional Review Board approval. After weight-based ^{82}Rb injection, the list-mode data of each scan for the first 6 min and 10 s were rebinned into 27 dynamic frames (14×5 s, 6×10 s, 3×20 s, 3×30 s, 1×90 s), resulting in a total of 2210 early-to-late pairs. The details of the imaging and reconstruction protocol are in Supplementary Figure S1. In all the scans, the rough segmentations of RVBP, LVBP, and myocardium were manually labeled with reference to the last dynamic frame for TAC generation and the following MBF quantification.

2.2   Network Architecture

The structure of the proposed network TAI-GAN is shown in Fig. 1. The generator predicts the related late frame using the input early frame, with the backbone structure of a 3-D U-Net [5] (4 encoding and decoding levels), modified to be temporally and anatomically informed. The discriminator analyzes the true and generated late frames and categorizes them as either real or fake, employing the structure of PatchGAN [13] (3 encoding levels, 1 linear output layer).

Temporally Informed by Tracer Dynamics and FiLM. To address the high variation in tracer distribution in the different phases, the temporal information related to tracer dynamics is introduced to the network by concatenating RVBP and LVBP TACs as well as the frame temporal index in one-hot format. A long short-term memory (LSTM) [11] layer encodes the concatenated temporal input, and the following 1-D convolutional layer and linear layer map the LSTM outputs to the channel-wise parameters γ and β. The feature-wise linear modulation (FiLM) [19] layer then manipulates the bottleneck feature map by the generated scaling factor γ and bias β, as in (1),

$$FiLM(M_i) = \gamma_i \cdot M_i + \beta_i, \tag{1}$$

where M_i is the ith channel of the bottleneck feature map, γ_i and β_i are the scaling factor and the bias of the ith channel, respectively.

Anatomically Informed by Segmentation Locators. The dual-channel input of the generator is the early frame concatenated with the rough segmentations of RVBP, LVBP, and myocardium. Note that cardiac segmentations are already required in MBF quantification and this is an essential part of the current clinical workflow. In our work, the labeled masks serve as the anatomical locator to inform the generator of the cardiac ROI location and prevent spatial mismatch in frame conversion. This is especially helpful in discriminating against the frame conversion of early RV and LV phases. Random local shifts of the segmentations are applied during training. This improves the robustness of the conversion network to motion between the early frame and the last frame.

Loss Function. Both an adversarial loss and a voxel-wise mean squared error (MSE) loss are included in the loss function of TAI-GAN, as in (2)–(4),

$$L_{adv} = -log(D(F_L)) - log(1 - D(G(F_i))) \tag{2}$$

$$L_{mse} = \frac{1}{V} \sum_{n=1}^{V} (G(F_i)_n - (F_L)_n)^2 \tag{3}$$

$$\hat{G}, \hat{D} = arg \min_G \max_D (L_{adv} + L_{mse}) \tag{4}$$

where L_{adv} is the adversarial loss, L_{mse} is the MSE loss, D is the discriminator, G is the generator, F_L is the real last frame, $G(F_i)$ is the generator-mapped last frame from the ith early frame F_i, and V is the number of voxels in each frame.

2.3   Network Training and Image Conversion Evaluation

All the early frames with LVBP activity higher than 10% of the maximum activity in TAC are converted to the last frame. Very early frames with lower activity in LVBP are not considered as they do not have a meaningful impact on the image-derived input function and subsequently the associated MBF quantification [22]. Prior to model input, all the frames were individually normalized to the intensity range of $[-1,1]$. Patch-based training was implemented with a random cropping size of (64,64,32) near the location of LV inferior wall center, random rotation in the xy plane with the range of $[-45°,45°]$, and 3-D random translation with the range of $[-5,5]$ voxels as the data augmentation.

Considering the low feasibility of training each one-to-one mapping for all the early frames, we trained two pairwise mappings using a vanilla GAN (3-D U-Net generator) and solely the adversarial loss as a comparison with the state-of-the-art method by Sundar et al. [24]. The two specific mappings are one frame before and one frame after the EQ frame, the first frame when LVBP activity is equal to or higher than RVBP activity [22], respectively EQ-1 and EQ+1.

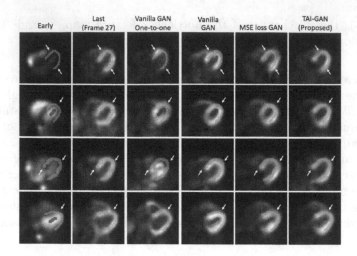

Fig. 2. Sample early-to-late frame conversion results of each method with overlaid segmentations of RVBP (red), LVBP (blue), and myocardium (green). (Color figure online)

We also implemented the vanilla GAN and the MSE loss GAN as two all-to-one conversion baselines. A preliminary ablation study of the introduced temporal and anatomic information is summarized in Supplementary Figure S2 and Table S1. A comparison of the average training time and memory footprint is included in Supplementary Table S2.

All the deep learning models are developed using PyTorch and trained under 5-fold cross-validation on an NVIDIA A40 GPU using Adam optimizer (learning rate $G = 2e-4$, $D = 5e-5$). In each fold, 17 scans were randomly selected as the test set and the remaining 68 were for training. The stopping epoch was 800 for one-to-one mappings and 100 for all the all-to-one models.

Image conversion evaluations include visualizing the generated last frames against the real last frame and the input frame, with overlaid cardiac segmentations. Quantitatively, the MSE, normalized mean absolute error (NMAE), peak signal-to-noise ratio (PSNR), and structural similarity index (SSIM) are computed between the generated and real last frames. Differences between methods were assessed by fold-wise paired two-tailed t-tests ($\alpha = 0.05$).

2.4 Motion Correction and Clinical MBF Quantification

Since all the included scans are categorized as motion-free, we ran a motion simulation test to evaluate the benefit of frame conversion on motion correction using the test set of one random fold, resulting in 17 cases. On an independent ^{82}Rb cardiac scan cohort identified as having significant motion by the clinical team, we ran non-rigid motion correction in BioImage Suite [14] (BIS) to generate motion fields. We applied the motion field estimations from the late frames scaled by 2 to the motion-free test frames as motion ground-truth. In

Table 1. Quantitative image similarity evaluation of early-to-late frame conversion (mean ± standard deviation) with the best results marked **in bold**.

Test set	Metric	Vanilla GAN One-to-one	Vanilla GAN	MSE loss GAN	TAI-GAN(Proposed)
EQ-1	SSIM	0.557 ± 0.017*	0.640 ± 0.021	0.633 ± 0.053*	0.657 ± 0.018
	MSE	0.057 ± 0.001*	0.050 ± 0.006*	0.044 ± 0.011	0.040 ± 0.005
	NMAE	0.068 ± 0.002*	0.063 ± 0.005*	0.059 ± 0.009	0.057 ± 0.005
	PSNR	18.678 ± 0.116*	19.370 ± 0.474*	19.950 ± 0.949	**20.335 ± 0.530**
EQ+1	SSIM	0.669 ± 0.061*	0.679 ± 0.014	0.680 ± 0.011	**0.691 ± 0.013**
	MSE	0.032 ± 0.014	0.034 ± 0.002	0.033 ± 0.006	**0.032 ± 0.002**
	NMAE	0.050 ± 0.011	0.053 ± 0.003	0.051 ± 0.006	**0.048 ± 0.003**
	PSNR	21.323 ± 1.800	21.014 ± 0.355	21.188 ± 0.757	**21.361 ± 0.205**
All Pre-EQ frames	SSIM	–	0.594 ± 0.012*	0.596 ± 0.047*	**0.627 ± 0.025**
	MSE	–	0.063 ± 0.010*	0.053 ± 0.016	**0.046 ± 0.009**
	NMAE	–	0.072 ± 0.007*	0.066 ± 0.011	**0.062 ± 0.008**
	PSNR	–	18.507 ± 0.474*	19.269 ± 1.036*	**19.834 ± 0.738**
All frames	SSIM	–	0.708 ± 0.010*	0.716 ± 0.007*	**0.733 ± 0.018**
	MSE	–	0.027 ± 0.002*	0.024 ± 0.003	**0.021 ± 0.002**
	NMAE	–	0.047 ± 0.004*	0.044 ± 0.002	**0.040 ± 0.002**
	PSNR	–	22.803 ± 0.530*	23.241 ± 0.342*	**23.799 ± 0.466**

*P < 0.05 between the current class and TAI-GAN (subject-wise paired two-tailed t-test).

this way, the characteristics of simulated motion match with real-patient motion and also have significant magnitudes. The different image conversion methods were applied to the early frames prior to motion simulation. All original and converted frames with simulated motion were then registered to the last frame using BIS with the settings as in [8]. We calculated the mean absolute prediction error to measure motion prediction accuracy,

$$|\Delta\Phi| = \frac{1}{P} \sum_{n=1}^{P} \frac{|\Phi_{x_n} - \hat{\Phi}_{x_n}| + |\Phi_{y_n} - \hat{\Phi}_{y_n}| + |\Phi_{z_n} - \hat{\Phi}_{z_n}|}{3}, \tag{5}$$

where P is the number of transformation control points in a frame, $(\hat{\Phi}_{x_n}, \hat{\Phi}_{y_n}, \hat{\Phi}_{z_n})$ is the motion prediction, and $(\Phi_{x_n}, \Phi_{y_n}, \Phi_{z_n})$ is the motion ground-truth.

After motion estimation, the predicted motion of each method is applied to the original frames without intensity normalization for kinetic modeling. To estimate the uptake rate K_1, the LVBP TAC as the image-derived input function and myocardium TAC were fitted to a 1-tissue compartment model using weighted least squares fitting as in [23]. MBF was then calculated from K_1 under the relationship as in [7]. The percentage differences of K_1 and MBF were calculated between the motion-free ground-truth and motion-corrected values. The weighted sum-of-squared residuals were computed between the MBF model predictions and the observed TACs. We also included a comparison of LVBP and myocardium TACs in Supplementary Figure S3.

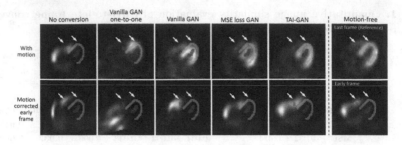

Fig. 3. Sample motion simulation and correction results with different methods of frame conversion.

3   Results

3.1   Frame Conversion Performance

The sample results of the early-to-late frame conversion by each method are visualized in Fig. 2. Although the one-to-one models were trained under the most specific temporal mapping, the prediction results were not satisfactory and showed some failure cases, possibly due to the small sample size and the insufficient kinetics information of a given early frame. Among the all-to-one models, vanilla GAN was able to learn the conversion patterns but with some distortions. After introducing MSE loss, the GAN generated results with higher visual similarity. After introducing temporal and anatomical information, the visual performance of the proposed TAI-GAN was the best with less mismatch and distortion.

The image similarity evaluation results are summarized in Table 1. Note that the similarity is quantitatively compared between the normalized predicted and real last frames as the intermediate conversion results, not representing actual tracer concentrations. The one-to-one training pair did not achieve better results than the all-to-one models, possibly due to the lack of inter-frame tracer dynamic dependencies. The TAI-GAN achieved the best result in each metric on each test set. The major improvement of the proposed TAI-GAN was for the Pre-EQ frames where the LVBP activity < RVBP activity, which is the most challenging to convert to late frame due to the large difference between the input and output frames.

3.2   Motion Correction Evaluation

Sample motion simulation and correction results are shown in Fig. 3. The simulated non-rigid motion introduced distortion to the frames and the mismatch between the motion-affected early frame and the segmentation is observed. After directly registering the original frames, the resliced frame was even more deformed, likely due to the tracer distribution differences in the registration pair. Early-to-late frame conversion could address such challenging registration cases,

Table 2. Mean absolute motion prediction errors without and with each conversion method (in mm, mean ± standard deviation) with the best results marked **in bold**.

	No Conversion	Vanilla GAN One-to-one	Vanilla GAN	MSE loss GAN	TAI-GAN
All frames	4.45 ± 0.64*	–	4.40 ± 0.49*	4.76 ± 0.48*	**3.48 ± 0.45**
EQ-1	6.18 ± 1.51*	5.33 ± 1.34	6.03 ± 1.06*	5.12 ± 0.72*	**5.06 ± 0.78**
EQ+1	5.12 ± 0.93*	4.72 ± 0.86	4.93 ± 0.80*	4.81 ± 0.46*	**4.35 ± 0.87**

*$P < 0.05$ between the current class and TAI-GAN (paired-wise paired two-tailed t-test).

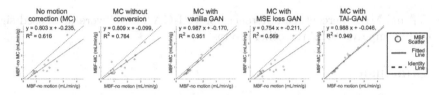

Fig. 4. Scatter plots of MBF results estimated from motion-free frames vs. no motion correction (MC) and motion correction after different conversion methods.

but additional mismatches might be introduced due to conversion errors, as seen in the vanilla and MSE loss GAN results. With minimal local distortion and the highest frame similarity, the conversion result of the proposed TAI-GAN matched the myocardium and ventricle locations with the original early frame and the registration result demonstrated the best visual alignment.

Table 2 summarizes the mean absolute motion prediction error on the original early frames and converted frames. Generally, the early acquisition time of a frame relates to high motion prediction errors. In all the included early frames and both EQ-1 and EQ+1 frames, the proposed TAI-GAN achieved the lowest motion prediction error and significantly reduced average prediction error compared to no conversion and all-to-one GAN models ($p < 0.05$). The improvement of motion correction accuracy after proper frame conversion is suggested.

3.3 Parametric Fitting and Clinical MBF Quantification

Figure 4 shows the scatter plots of MBF results estimated from motion-free frames vs. no motion correction and motion correction after different conversion approaches. With simulated motion, the MBF estimates were mostly lower than the ground-truth. The fitted line of motion correction with vanilla GAN was closer to the identity line compared with motion correction without conversion. The fitted line of motion correction with MSE loss GAN was next to that of no motion correction with a slight correction effect. The fitted line of motion correction with the proposed TAI-GAN was the closest to the identity line, suggesting the most improvement in MBF quantification.

Table 3 summarizes the bias of K_1 and MBF as well as the parametric fitting error. The fitting error of TAI-GAN+MC was the lowest among all the test classes and didn't show a significant difference with the motion-free error ($p > 0.05$).

Table 3. K_1 and MBF quantification results (mean ± standard deviation) with the best results marked **in bold**.

	Mean K_1 percentage difference (%)	Mean MBF percentage difference (%)	Mean K_1 fitting error ($\times 10^{-5}$)
Motion-free	–	–	3.07 ± 1.85
With motion	$-25.97 \pm 18.05^*$	$-36.99 \pm 23.37^*$	$10.08 \pm 8.70^\dagger$
Motion corrected (MC)	$-17.76 \pm 19.51^*$	$-25.09 \pm 31.71^*$	$22.18 \pm 24.24^\dagger$
Vanilla GAN+MC	$-11.09 \pm 9.79^*$	$-16.93 \pm 14.84^*$	$7.72 \pm 6.64^\dagger$
MSE loss GAN+MC	$-27.99 \pm 18.61^*$	$-39.52 \pm 23.89^*$	$13.05 \pm 13.16^\dagger$
TAI-GAN+MC	$\mathbf{-5.07 \pm 7.68}$	$\mathbf{-7.95 \pm 11.99}$	$\mathbf{3.80 \pm 3.00}$

The K_1 and MBF percentage differences of TAI-GAN+MC were decreased significantly compared to all the other groups.

4   Conclusion

We propose TAI-GAN, a temporally and anatomically informed GAN for early-to-late frame conversion to aid dynamic cardiac PET motion correction. The TAI-GAN can successfully perform early-to-late frame conversion with desired visual results and high quantitative similarity to the real last frames. Frame conversion by TAI-GAN can aid conventional image registration for motion estimation and subsequently achieve accurate motion correction and MBF estimation. Future work includes the evaluation of deep learning motion correction methods and real patient motion as well as the validation of clinical impact using invasive catheterization as the clinical gold standard.

Acknowledgements. This work is supported under National Institutes of Health (NIH) grant R01 CA224140.

References

1. Ak, K.E., Lim, J.H., Tham, J.Y., Kassim, A.A.: Semantically consistent text to fashion image synthesis with an enhanced attentional generative adversarial network. Pattern Recogn. Lett. **135**, 22–29 (2020)
2. Ak, K.E., Lim, J.H., Tham, J.Y., Kassim, A.: Semantically consistent hierarchical text to fashion image synthesis with an enhanced-attentional generative adversarial network. In: 2019 IEEE/CVF International Conference on Computer Vision Workshop (ICCVW), pp. 3121–3124. IEEE (2019)
3. Burckhardt, D.D.: Cardiac positron emission tomography: overview of myocardial perfusion, myocardial blood flow and coronary flow reserve imaging. Mol. Imag. (2009)
4. Cao, X., Yang, J., Gao, Y., Wang, Q., Shen, D.: Region-adaptive deformable registration of CT/MRI pelvic images via learning-based image synthesis. IEEE Trans. Image Process. **27**(7), 3500–3512 (2018)
5. Çiçek, Ö., Abdulkadir, A., Lienkamp, S.S., Brox, T., Ronneberger, O.: 3D U-Net: learning dense volumetric segmentation from sparse annotation. In: Ourselin, S., Joskowicz, L., Sabuncu, M.R., Unal, G., Wells, W. (eds.) MICCAI 2016. LNCS, vol. 9901, pp. 424–432. Springer, Cham (2016). https://doi.org/10.1007/978-3-319-46723-8_49

6. Dey, N., Ren, M., Dalca, A.V., Gerig, G.: Generative adversarial registration for improved conditional deformable templates. In: Proceedings of the IEEE/CVF International Conference on Computer Vision, pp. 3929–3941 (2021)
7. Germino, M., et al.: Quantification of myocardial blood flow with 82 RB: validation with 15 O-water using time-of-flight and point-spread-function modeling. EJNMMI Res. **6**, 1–12 (2016)
8. Guo, X., et al.: Inter-pass motion correction for whole-body dynamic PET and parametric imaging. IEEE Trans. Radiat. Plasma Med. Sci. **7**, 344–353 (2022)
9. Guo, X., Zhou, B., Chen, X., Liu, C., Dvornek, N.C.: MCP-Net: inter-frame motion correction with Patlak regularization for whole-body dynamic pet. In: Wang, L., Dou, Q., Fletcher, P.T., Speidel, S., Li, S. (eds.) MICCAI 2022. LNCS, vol. 13434, pp. 163–172. Springer, Cham (2022). https://doi.org/10.1007/978-3-031-16440-8_16
10. Guo, X., Zhou, B., Pigg, D., Spottiswoode, B., Casey, M.E., Liu, C., Dvornek, N.C.: Unsupervised inter-frame motion correction for whole-body dynamic pet using convolutional long short-term memory in a convolutional neural network. Med. Image Anal. **80**, 102524 (2022). https://doi.org/10.1016/j.media.2022.102524
11. Hochreiter, S., Schmidhuber, J.: Long short-term memory. Neural Comput. **9**(8), 1735–1780 (1997)
12. Hunter, C.R., Klein, R., Beanlands, R.S., deKemp, R.A.: Patient motion effects on the quantification of regional myocardial blood flow with dynamic pet imaging. Med. Phys. **43**(4), 1829–1840 (2016)
13. Isola, P., Zhu, J.Y., Zhou, T., Efros, A.A.: Image-to-image translation with conditional adversarial networks. In: Proceedings of the IEEE Conference on Computer Vision and Pattern Recognition, pp. 1125–1134 (2017)
14. Joshi, A., et al.: Unified framework for development, deployment and robust testing of neuroimaging algorithms. Neuroinformatics **9**(1), 69–84 (2011)
15. Liu, X., Jiang, D., Wang, M., Song, Z.: Image synthesis-based multi-modal image registration framework by using deep fully convolutional networks. Med. Biol. Eng. Comput. **57**, 1037–1048 (2019)
16. Lu, Y., Liu, C.: Patient motion correction for dynamic cardiac pet: current status and challenges. J. Nucl. Cardiol. **27**, 1999–2002 (2020)
17. Mao, X., Chen, Y., Li, Y., Xiong, T., He, Y., Xue, H.: Bilinear representation for language-based image editing using conditional generative adversarial networks. In: ICASSP 2019–2019 IEEE International Conference on Acoustics, Speech and Signal Processing (ICASSP), pp. 2047–2051. IEEE (2019)
18. Maul, J., Said, S., Ruiter, N., Hopp, T.: X-ray synthesis based on triangular mesh models using GPU-accelerated ray tracing for multi-modal breast image registration. In: Svoboda, D., Burgos, N., Wolterink, J.M., Zhao, C. (eds.) SASHIMI 2021. LNCS, vol. 12965, pp. 87–96. Springer, Cham (2021). https://doi.org/10.1007/978-3-030-87592-3_9
19. Perez, E., Strub, F., De Vries, H., Dumoulin, V., Courville, A.: FiLM: visual reasoning with a general conditioning layer. In: Proceedings of the AAAI Conference on Artificial Intelligence, vol. 32 (2018)
20. Prior, J.O., et al.: Quantification of myocardial blood flow with 82 RB positron emission tomography: clinical validation with 15 O-water. Eur. J. Nucl. Med. Mol. Imaging **39**, 1037–1047 (2012)
21. Rachmadi, M.F., del C. Valdés-Hernández, M., Makin, S., Wardlaw, J.M., Komura, T.: Predicting the evolution of white matter hyperintensities in brain MRI using generative adversarial networks and irregularity map. In: Shen, D., et al. (eds.)

MICCAI 2019. LNCS, vol. 11766, pp. 146–154. Springer, Cham (2019). https://doi.org/10.1007/978-3-030-32248-9_17

22. Shi, L., et al.: Automatic inter-frame patient motion correction for dynamic cardiac pet using deep learning. IEEE Trans. Med. Imaging **40**, 3293–3304 (2021)

23. Shi, L., et al.: Direct list mode parametric reconstruction for dynamic cardiac SPECT. IEEE Trans. Med. Imaging **39**(1), 119–128 (2019)

24. Sundar, L.K.S., et al.: Conditional generative adversarial networks aided motion correction of dynamic 18F-FDG PET brain studies. J. Nucl. Med. **62**(6), 871–879 (2021)

25. Sundar, L.S., et al.: Data-driven motion compensation using cGAN for total-body [18F] FDG-PET imaging (2021)

26. Woo, J., et al.: Automatic 3D registration of dynamic stress and rest 82Rb and flurpiridaz F 18 myocardial perfusion PET data for patient motion detection and correction. Med. Phys. **38**(11), 6313–6326 (2011)

27. Zhou, B., et al.: Fast-MC-PET: a novel deep learning-aided motion correction and reconstruction framework for accelerated PET. In: Frangi, A., de Bruijne, M., Wassermann, D., Navab, N. (eds.) IPMI 2023. LNCS, vol. 13939, pp. 523–535. Springer, Cham (2023). https://doi.org/10.1007/978-3-031-34048-2_40

How Good Are Synthetic Medical Images? An Empirical Study with Lung Ultrasound

Menghan Yu[1,2], Sourabh Kulhare[1]([✉]), Courosh Mehanian[1],
Charles B. Delahunt[1], Daniel E. Shea[1], Zohreh Laverriere[1], Ishan Shah[1],
and Matthew P. Horning[1]

[1] Global Health Labs, Inc, Bellevue, WA 98004, USA
{sourabh.kulhare,menghan.yu}@ghlabs.org
[2] University of Washington, Seattle, WA 98105, USA

Abstract. Acquiring large quantities of data and annotations is effective for developing high-performing deep learning models, but is difficult and expensive to do in the healthcare context. Adding synthetic training data using generative models offers a low-cost method to deal effectively with the data scarcity challenge, and can also address data imbalance and patient privacy issues. In this study, we propose a comprehensive framework that fits seamlessly into model development workflows for medical image analysis. We demonstrate, with datasets of varying size, (i) the benefits of generative models as a data augmentation method; (ii) how adversarial methods can protect patient privacy via data substitution; (iii) novel performance metrics for these use cases by testing models on real holdout data. We show that training with both synthetic and real data outperforms training with real data alone, and that models trained solely with synthetic data approach their real-only counterparts. Code is available at https://github.com/Global-Health-Labs/US-DCGAN.

1 Introduction

The great successes of deep learning have depended on massive datasets with ground truth labels provided by domain experts. But in the healthcare context, the amount of data available for model development is often limited due to privacy, security, legal, cost, and resource availability issues. The latter two are especially challenging in low-resource settings, such as low- and middle-income countries (LMIC). Negative cases are usually easily obtainable but the paucity of positive cases can be a bottleneck, especially for rare conditions.

Various methods have been proposed to address data scarcity. Here, we explore the use of Generative Adversarial Networks (GANs), introduced by Goodfellow *et al.* [5], which generate synthetic images that closely resemble

Supplementary Information The online version contains supplementary material available at https://doi.org/10.1007/978-3-031-44689-4_8.

J. M. Wolterink et al. (Eds.): SASHIMI 2023, LNCS 14288, pp. 75–85, 2023.
https://doi.org/10.1007/978-3-031-44689-4_8

images in a particular domain. This raises the intriguing possibility of using synthetic images in a medical context to simultaneously address scarcity, class imbalance, and privacy concerns. Synthetic images with and without the feature of interest can be generated, which can both balance classes and increase the total number of samples. Furthermore, synthetic images are not traceable to any specific patient, being based on a random vector, thus maintaining patient privacy.

Recently, a number of works [3,4,11,13] have applied generative algorithms in the medical image domain. Hu *et al.* [7] explored using conditional GANs to simulate fetal ultrasound images at a given 3D spatial location relative to the patient's anatomy. SpeckleGAN [1] integrates a network module with speckle noise into a GAN architecture to generate realistic intravascular ultrasound (IVUS) images. Other studies illustrate the effectiveness of GANs in generating synthetic breast ultrasound [6,15], thyroid ultrasound [12], and transcranial focused ultrasound [8], showcasing their utility in various applications. Deep Convolutional Generative Adversarial Networks (DCGAN) [16] has emerged as a important building block of many generative approaches.

Despite notable advances in generating synthetic images using GANs, quantitative performance evaluation remains underdeveloped. Many of the current evaluation methods rely on subjective visual inspection, which makes it challenging in medical domains like ultrasound that require radiology expertise. Xu *et al.* [21] enumerate existing quantitative metrics and discuss their strengths and limitations. While these metrics are an improvement over subjective evaluations, they do not measure the usefulness of synthetically generated images for a downstream task. In our evaluation of GAN performance, we go beyond metrics that evaluate distributional characteristics. We also assess their performance for a clinically relevant downstream task.

To show the feasibility of this approach, we develop a comprehensive framework for synthetic image generation that fits seamlessly into model development workflows for medical image analysis. Concretely, we apply the framework to pneumonia, which remains a major global health concern. While pneumonia is no longer a problem in rich countries, it remains the leading cause of child mortality in LMICs [20]. Accurate and timely diagnosis of pediatric pneumonia can expedite treatment and potentially save children's lives.

The standard-of-care for confirmatory imaging in high-income countries is X-ray, which is often not an option in LMICs. Lung ultrasound has emerged as a promising alternative with many advantages including safety, portability, and low cost. However, confirming pneumonia with lung ultrasound is challenging because images mainly consist of acoustic artifacts whose interpretation requires expertise, which is lacking in LMICs. Deep learning has proved to be an effective tool to assist healthcare workers to identify lung ultrasound features associated with pneumonia [10,14,17], the primary one being consolidation (see Fig. 1).

Our contributions are as follows:

- We apply DCGAN to generate synthetic images for a medically high-impact downstream task: consolidation classification. To the best of our knowledge, our work represents the first application of DCGAN to lung ultrasound.
- We present novel quantitative metrics that measure real and synthetic image distribution similarity and the presence of image features of interest.
- We show the benefit of synthetic data in two crucial use cases: augmentation of scarce data, and protection of patient privacy via data substitution.

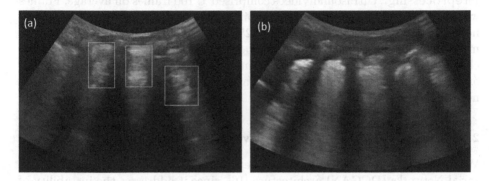

Fig. 1. Consolidation in lung ultrasound. (a) Real consolidation image: infection-induced inflammation causes fluid buildup in the alveoli, presenting as hyper- and hypo-echoic splotches (yellow boxes). (b) Synthetic consolidation image. (Color figure online)

2 Methods

2.1 Dataset

Description and Collection Process. A study conducted from 2017–2022 in Nigeria collected lung ultrasound data at three sites comprising 550 pediatric patients (*i.e.*, < 18 years old, 29% female, 71% male). The data has been described previously [17]. Briefly, ultrasound cine loops were collected (with the Mindray DP-10 with 35C50EB curvilinear probe) from 10 lung zones covering anterior, lateral, and posterior locations consistent with the international lung ultrasound protocol [19]. Radiology (X-ray) of the lungs was performed prior to the ultrasound exam and, combined with clinical indications, was used to screen patients and identify ground truth diagnosis. Table 1 lists patient, video, and frame counts across training, validation, and holdout sets. For negative patients, all videos without consolidation (possibly containing other abnormal features) were included. For positive patients, in contrast, only videos exhibiting consolidation were included. The supplement provides details on device settings, data collection protocol, and patient demographics.

Annotation Process. Ultrasound data were annotated at both the video and frame levels using a custom web-based tool. Annotations were performed by expert lung ultrasound physicians to identify the following lung features: pleural line, A-line, B-line, merged B-line, abnormal pleural line, pleural effusion, and consolidation [2]. For this work, videos with consolidation were used as feature positive videos and videos with no consolidation were used as negative videos. Frame annotations were used as ground truth for feature-positive frames to train and evaluate CNN classifiers.

Preprocessing. Ultrasound videos comprised $\gtrsim 100$ frames on average. Frames were centrally cropped using fixed cropping points and masked to remove extraneous text. Frames were resized to 256×256 and pixel values standardized to zero mean and unit standard deviation for both image generation and downstream classification tasks. To ensure clean frame labels, positive frames were selected only from consolidation-positive videos, and negative frames from consolidation-negative videos.

2.2   Deep Convolutional Generative Adversarial Networks

We use a backbone network similar to the Deep Convolutional Generative Adversarial Networks (DCGAN) architecture [16], since it addresses the instability of vanilla GANs and allows arbitrary output image resolution. The input tensor size of the discriminator and the output of the generator were set to $256 \times 256 \times 1$, which is fine enough to capture lung ultrasound details and enables the use of off-the-shelf pre-trained models [9] to evaluate synthetic images. The generator consists of a cascade of strided 2D transposed convolutional layers, batch normalizations, and ReLu activations, with an input latent vector $\mathbf{z}$ that is drawn from a standard normal distribution. The discriminator comprises a cascade of 2D strided convolutional layers, batch normalization layers, and leaky ReLu activations. We stabilized the adversarial training process by using a smaller batch size of 16, lowering generator and discriminator learning rates (1×10^{-5} and 5×10^{-6} respectively), and adding a dropout layer (rate 0.25) after each convolutional block of the discriminator. Full details can be found in the code.

Table 1. Counts of negative and positive patients, videos, and frames, in training, validation, and testing sets, which were defined at the patient level.

Pediatric	Training		Validation		Testing	
	neg	pos	neg	pos	neg	pos
Patients	122	134	23	96	24	100
Videos	5,022	1,134	1,229	404	695	423
Frames	426,675	99,134	163,705	58,580	117,391	64,955

2.3 Evaluations

Qualitative Metrics. Synthesized images are assessed for the presence of features commonly observed in lung ultrasound. Details are described in Sect. 3.

Quantitative Metrics. We adopt three metrics to monitor GAN convergence during training, choose the best GAN model, and evaluate image quality. Following [21], we use (i) kernel Maximum Mean Discrepancy (kMMD), which measures the distance between the real and synthetic image distributions. At every GAN training epoch, we randomly sample 2,000 images from the training set and use the current GAN model to randomly generate 2,000 synthetic images. We estimate kMMD empirically over image pairs from both sets. If real and synthetic distributions closely match, mean kMMD should be near zero.

Also following [21], we use (ii) a 1-Nearest Neighbor (1NN) classifier to distinguish real and synthetic positive images, which is trained and evaluated in a leave-one-out (LOO) fashion. Zero accuracy indicates overfitting to the real image distribution, while unit accuracy means perfect separability, indicating non-overlap between the real and generated distributions. Ideally, 1NN accuracy should be near 0.5 (*i.e.*, chance). For (i) and (ii), images are represented by the feature embedding generated by an ImageNet pre-trained ResNet34 model to ensure that meaningful image structural information is captured. Feature space image representation is described in more detail in the supplement.

Finally, we use (iii) a CNN consolidation classifier, trained in advance on real samples, to assess the presence (absence) of consolidation in synthetic positive (negative) images. For positive GAN training, average confidence scores near unity verify that consolidation features are present in the images, whereas for negative GAN training, confidence scores near zero indicate the absence of consolidation. The workflow for GAN training and evaluation is shown in Fig. 2.

Downstream Task Evaluations. We envision two scenarios: synthetic data can either augment or entirely replace training data. To evaluate the effectiveness of synthetic data in a realistic downstream task, we train CNNs for binary consolidation classification on a frame-by-frame basis and assess frame-level performance as a function of the amount of real training data used. The output of these consolidation CNNs is a confidence score and the relevant performance metric is the AUC-ROC performance on real hold-out test data.

Four classifiers with identical CNN architectures (reduced VGG [18]) are trained to recognize consolidation, with various positive and negative training sets as follows: Baseline classifier (iv) is trained with real positive and negative frames. Combined classifier (v) uses both synthetic and real positive frames and real negative frames. Positive synthetic classifier (vi) uses synthetic positive frames and real negative frames. Pure synthetic classifier (vii) uses only synthetic images for both positive and negative sets. All classifiers were trained under consistent "best known" practices: standard data augmentation techniques applied to training data, including horizontal flipping, gamma brightness adjustment,

Gaussian blurring, and random pixel intensity adjustment. We also did extensive hyper-parameter optimization (using random search to tune learning rate, channel multiplier, and dropout rate). Only the model with the highest validation accuracy is selected for evaluation on the holdout set.

3   Results

3.1   Qualitative Evaluation

Lung ultrasound images largely consist of artifacts generated by acoustic impedance mismatches between lung tissue, fluid, and air. To the trained eye, these artifacts convey information about lung pathologies such as consolidation, which manifests as sub-pleural hyper- and hypo-echoic splotches caused by inflammatory alveolar fluid buildup. See Fig. 1. We observe that the synthetic

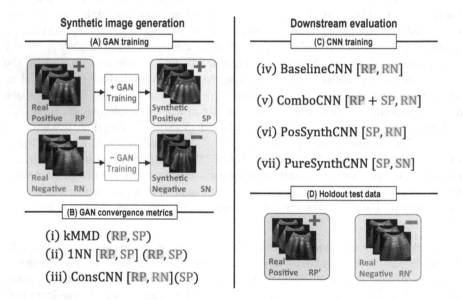

Fig. 2. GAN training and evaluation workflow. (A) Positive and negative GANs are trained with real positive and negative images, respectively. (B) Quantitative metrics monitor convergence during GAN training (Fig. 4). Square brackets indicate training sets; parentheses testing sets. (i) kMMD (no training) measures distance between real and synthetic distributions. (ii) 1-NN is trained to distinguish real and synthetic images and is tested in leave-one-out-fashion. (iii) Consolidation CNN is trained to recognize consolidation and is tested on synthetic images. (C) Downstream evaluations measure GAN effectiveness by training various CNNs and testing on real holdout data (Fig. 5). (iv) Baseline CNN is trained on real positive and negative images. (v) Combo-CNN is trained on real and synthetic positive images and real negative images. (vi) Positive synthetic CNN is trained on synthetic positive and real negative images. (vii) Pure synthetic CNN is trained on synthetic positive and negative images. (D) Holdout set of real positive and negative images is used for downstream CNN testing.

images also display such features and artifacts and preserve the architecture of lung ultrasound images. Figure 3 shows examples of synthetic and real, consolidated and normal, lung ultrasound images. Prominent features of lung ultrasound include the "bat sign" [2] and "rib shadows", caused by the pleural line and the impenetrability of ribs to ultrasound. These can be observed in the real and synthetic lung images (r1–r4, s1–s4). Pleural lines, A-lines (multiple-echo artifacts of the pleural line) are also present and qualitatively similar in synthetic images (r3, s3). The "shadows" on the left and right sides of images (r1, r2, r4, s1–s4) are caused by poor acoustic contact between the edges of the curvilinear transducer and the child's body, which is another realistic element of the the synthetic images. Other features of lung ultrasound also appear in synthetic images, such as "hepatization", caused by excessive fluid accumulation, as seen in (s1, s2). Additional synthetic examples are provided in the supplement.

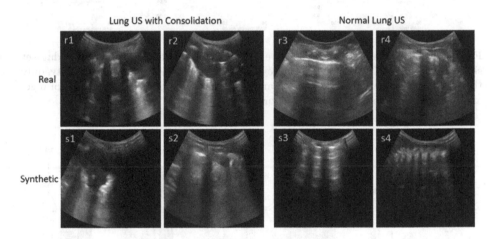

Fig. 3. Examples of real and synthetic images.

3.2 Quantitative Evaluation

Figure 4 plots quantitative evaluation metrics (kMMD, 1NN LOO accuracy, and $1-$ mean consolidation score as described in Sect. 2.3) for different training set sizes as a function of GAN training epoch. All metrics decreased over the course of training as expected and plateaued near 60 epochs. For the consolidation classifier, the mean score reached 0.96 for all training set sizes, indicating the success of synthesizing the consolidation feature. We note that although kMMD and 1NN accuracy did not reach their ideal levels, downstream classifiers trained using synthetic images generated with GAN models from epoch ≥ 60 performed acceptably well, indicating the utility of the quantitative metrics described here.

3.3 Downstream Evaluation

Figure 5 shows downstream results for different amounts of training data (patient counts of 6, 15, 29, 44, and 58). AUC-ROC on a holdout set containing only real images is plotted. Balanced positive and negative frame counts were maintained during the patient sampling process. The figure displays three bars for each dataset size: (iv) blue for the baseline model trained solely on real data, (v) green for the model trained by augmenting positives with synthetic data, and (vi) yellow for the model trained on synthetic data as proxy for positive data (as described in Sect. 2.3). To ensure robustness, each data ablation point was averaged over three random patient sampling replicates.

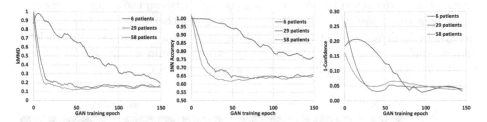

Fig. 4. Quantitative metrics for positive GAN training vs epoch for different dataset sizes. Left: kMMD. Center: 1NN accuracy. Right: 1− confidence score. For clarity, only three training set sizes are shown; 6, 29, and 58 patients are represented by blue, orange, and green lines, respectively. (Color figure online)

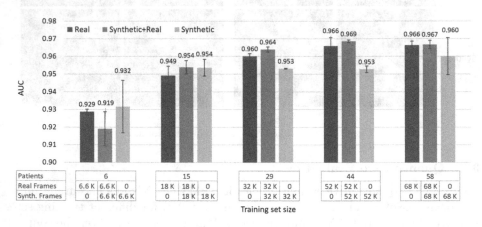

Fig. 5. Downstream evaluation results on real holdout test set for models trained as follows: blue: real only (baseline); green: real augmented with synthetic positive images; orange: synthetic positive images only. Green improvement over blue shows the benefit of synthetic augmentation. Approximate equivalence between orange and blue shows that synthetic data is a good proxy for real data. (Color figure online)

Our results highlight an advantage in training models by combining real patient data with GAN-generated synthetic data (except with very sparse training data). This can be seen as the improvement between the green and blue bars in Fig. 5 for training dataset size ≥ 15 patients, where the AUC-ROC averaged over replicates increased from 0.949 to 0.954. At this dataset size and greater, the GAN can generate high-quality consolidation ultrasound images that effectively cover the real data distribution.

Additionally, training models solely on synthetic positive images achieved comparable accuracy to models trained on real data only, as evidenced by the rough equivalence between the blue and orange bars in Fig. 5. This finding reduces the required amount of data to be collected and shared to develop high-performing models, thus mitigating privacy concerns and development costs.

Our work has primarily focused on generating feature-positive samples, which are often harder to obtain in a healthcare context. However, synthetic feature-negative samples are generated the same way, which are also useful for the patient privacy use case. This motivated the development of downstream task (vii) described in Sect. 2.3. For this model, the training set consists entirely of synthetic data, both positive and negative. The classifier thus trained achieved 92.2% accuracy and 0.962 AUC-ROC on the holdout set mentioned above.

4   Discussion

Deep learning has made tremendous strides in robust classification of medical images over the last decade and high-performing models are critical to using AI technology to address resource shortages in LMICs. But deep learning requires massive amounts of data to train clinically viable models. Generative adversarial networks have proved to be a useful tool in offsetting the amount of data required to train these models, thereby reducing cost and amplifying the impact of modest investments. At the same time, synthesized images can help to mitigate concern over patient privacy and balance data for rare conditions. These benefits improve the prospects for developing robust and unbiased models that can make a positive impact in healthcare in LMICs.

We have presented a framework for generating synthetic images and demonstrated its effectiveness using the healthcare-relevant example of consolidation in lung ultrasound images. Through a comprehensive suite of qualitative and quantitative assessment metrics, we have shown the model's proficiency in capturing the target distribution and the presence of the desired image features. Crucially, we have shown that synthetic data augmentation bolsters the performance of clinically relevant downstream tasks, which establishes the usefulness of synthetic images made with GANs.

Several research directions suggest themselves for future work. The first two convergence metrics are computed on image embeddings from a generic image classifier. Metrics based on ultrasound-specific embeddings, for example using contrastive self-supervised learning, would likely be more effective in this context. Furthermore, establishing correlation between metric values and downstream evaluations would be useful for assessing the value of those metrics. Finally, the statistical analysis of the results of blinded tests asking radiologists to distinguish between real and synthetic images would be instructive and complementary to the automated downstream evaluations.

Acknowledgements. We thank the Bill and Melinda Gates Foundation Trust for their generous support, and Xinliang Zheng, Ben Wilson, Meihua Zhu, Cynthia Gregory, and Kenton Gregory for their roles in managing the lung ultrasound project.

References

1. Bargsten, L., Schlaefer, A.: SpeckleGAN: a generative adversarial network with an adaptive speckle layer to augment limited training data for ultrasound image processing. IJCARS **15**, 1427–1436 (2020)
2. Bhoil, R., Ahluwalia, A., Chopra, R., Surya, M., Bhoil, S.: Signs and lines in lung ultrasound. J. Ultrason. **21**(86), 225–233 (2021)
3. Chuquicusma, M.J., et al.: How to fool radiologists with GANs? a visual turing test for lung cancer diagnosis. In: ISBI, pp. 240–244. IEEE (2018)
4. Frid-Adar, M., et al.: Synthetic data augmentation using GAN for improved liver lesion classification. In: ISBI, pp. 289–293. IEEE (2018)
5. Goodfellow, I., et al.: Generative adversarial networks. In: NeurIPS (2014)
6. Haq, D.Z., Fatichah, C.: Ultrasound image synthetic generating using deep convolution generative adversarial network for breast cancer identification. IPTEK J. Technol. Sci. **34**(1), 12 (2023)
7. Hu, Y., et al.: Freehand ultrasound image simulation with spatially-conditioned generative adversarial networks. In: Cardoso, M.J., et al. (eds.) CMMI/SWITCH/RAMBO -2017. LNCS, vol. 10555, pp. 105–115. Springer, Cham (2017). https://doi.org/10.1007/978-3-319-67564-0_11
8. Koh, H., et al.: Acoustic simulation for transcranial focused ultrasound using GAN-based synthetic CT. IEEE J. Biomed. Health Inform. **26**(1), 161–171 (2021)
9. Krizhevsky, A., Sutskever, I., Hinton, G.E.: ImageNet classification with deep convolutional neural networks. Commun. ACM **60**(6), 84–90 (2017)
10. Kulhare, S., et al.: Ultrasound-based detection of lung abnormalities using single shot detection convolutional neural networks. In: Stoyanov, D., et al. (eds.) POCUS/BIVPCS/CuRIOUS/CPM -2018. LNCS, vol. 11042, pp. 65–73. Springer, Cham (2018). https://doi.org/10.1007/978-3-030-01045-4_8
11. Lahiri, A., Ayush, K., Kumar Biswas, P., Mitra, P.: Generative adversarial learning for reducing manual annotation in semantic segmentation on large scale microscopy images: automated vessel segmentation in retinal fundus image as test case. In: Proceedings of CVPR Workshops, pp. 42–48 (2017)
12. Liang, J., Chen, J.: Data augmentation of thyroid ultrasound images using generative adversarial network. In: IEEE IUS, pp. 1–4. IEEE (2021)
13. Nie, D., et al.: Medical image synthesis with deep convolutional adversarial networks. IEEE TBME **65**(12), 2720–2730 (2018)
14. Ouyang, J., et al.: Weakly semi-supervised detection in lung ultrasound videos. In: IPMI 2023, pp. 195–207 (2023)
15. Pang, T., Wong, J.H.D., Ng, W.L., Chan, C.S.: Semi-supervised GAN-based radiomics model for data augmentation in breast ultrasound mass classification. Comput. Meth. Prog. Biomed. **203**, 106018 (2021)
16. Radford, A., et al.: Unsupervised representation learning with deep convolutional generative adversarial networks. arXiv preprint arXiv:1511.06434 (2015)
17. Shea, D., et al.: Deep learning video classification of lung ultrasound features associated with pneumonia. In: CVPR 2023, pp. 3102–3111. IEEE (2023)
18. Simonyan, K., Zisserman, A.: Very deep convolutional networks for large-scale image recognition. arXiv preprint arXiv:1409.1556 (2015)

19. Volpicelli, G., et al.: International evidence-based recommendations for point-of-care lung ultrasound. Int. J. Med. Inform. **129**, 413–422 (2019)
20. World Health Organization (WHO): Pneumonia (2016). https://www.who.int/mediacentre/factsheets/fs331/en
21. Xu, Q., et al.: An empirical study on evaluation metrics of generative adversarial networks. arXiv preprint arXiv:1806.07755 (2018)

Unsupervised Liver Tumor Segmentation with Pseudo Anomaly Synthesis

Zhaoxiang Zhang$^{(\boxtimes)}$, Hanqiu Deng , and Xingyu Li

University of Alberta, Edmonton, AB T6G 2R3, Canada
{zhaoxia2,hanqiu1,xingyu}@ualberta.ca

Abstract. Liver lesion segmentation is a challenging task. Liver lesions often appear as regional heterogeneity in various shapes and intensities, while collecting a comprehensive dataset for supervised learning is costly. To address this issue, this study formulates unsupervised liver tumor segmentation as an anomaly segmentation problem and presents a pseudo-supervised anomaly segmentation solution with synthetic anomalies. In this regard, we investigate two fundamental, yet under-explored questions: (1) how to generate anomalies? and (2) how to address a covariant shift between synthesis data and real tumor samples in model training? To the first question, instead of fabricating anomalies approximating the known abnormal patterns, we propose to generate anomalies spreading over a broader spectrum to encourage a model to learn the cluster boundary of normal samples. Our rationale toward the second question suggests light training on synthesis data for model generalizability. Based on these insights, this study incorporates a random-shaped anomaly synthesis module and two-stage training strategy into the DRAEM architecture for unsupervised liver tumor segmentation. Experiments on the public benchmark show that the proposed method trained on various synthetic anomalies has good generalizability on real tumor and achieves a comparable performance to prior arts. Our code is available at: https://github.com/nono-zz/LiTs-Segmentation.

Keywords: Lesion Segmentation · Unsupervised Learning · Anomaly Synthesis · Two-stage Training · CT

1 Introduction

Liver tumors are one of the leading causes of cancer-related deaths, and accurately segmenting them in medical images such as computed tomography (CT) is crucial for early detection and diagnosis. While supervised tumor segmentation methods show promising results, their performance is heavily dependent on high-quality annotated data, which can be expensive to obtain. Furthermore,

Supplementary Information The online version contains supplementary material available at https://doi.org/10.1007/978-3-031-44689-4_9.

due to the high heterogeneity of tumors, the generalizability of supervised models may be limited in identifying rare lesions or anomalies. Recently, there is an increased interest in treating tumors as anomalies in medical images and exploring unsupervised learning approaches, i.e. anomaly segmentation, to address the aforementioned challenges. In the context of unsupervised anomaly segmentation, a model is expected to identify and segment potential abnormalities by learning from a healthy cohort of patients during model training.

Prior arts in unsupervised anomaly segmentation can be categorized into two paradigms. The first paradigm stems from anomaly detection, where a model predicts if a query is normal or not and image regions that contribute most to this results are taken as the anomaly segmentation results. Among various anomaly detection methods, generative models, such as Variational Auto-Encoders (VAEs) [13], Generative Adversarial Networks (GANs) [8], Denoising Diffusion Probabilistic Models (DDPM) [9] have been extensively exploited [1,24,27,28,30,34]. Relying on the assumption that abnormal regions would be poorly reconstructed, the residue between the input and the generative model's output is used to detect abnormalities. Feature modelling in the embedding space is another approach. [5,23] employ the teacher-student architecture to extract features for normal and abnormal sample discrimination. [4,22] propose to detect the anomalies by out-of-distribution feature embedding. Despite their success in industrial anomaly detection [2], their effectiveness may be limited when applied to medical domain.

Alternative, anomaly synthesis has emerged as a prominent approach that incorporates pseudo-positive samples to enhance anomaly segmentation. By overlaying color, texture, and semantic outliers on normal samples, a model is trained to segment the synthetic anomalous regions [6,10,11,16,25,26,31,33]. Despite yielding promising results, there exists significant variation in methods for generating pseudo anomalies. For instance, [15,25,26] generate anomalies by utilizing in-distribution image patches, while [10,16,31,33] focus on producing lesions that closely resemble real anomalies. Additionally, prior arts usually focus on model design [16,32]. However, there is little study explicitly tackling the following two fundamental questions behind this paradigm.

- *Should pseudo-anomalies approximate the queries in the test phase?*
- *How should the segmentation model be trained on the synthesis data?*

In this study, we explore these questions and introduce two principles for pseudo-supervised anomaly segmentation with synthetic anomalies. We apply these principles to unsupervised liver tumor segmentation through adapted discriminative joint reconstruction anomaly embedding (DRAEM) [32]. Our approach introduces a varied anomaly synthesis pipeline and a balanced two-stage training strategy for DRAEM, resulting in outstanding performance on the liver tumor segmentation dataset (LiTs) [3].

2   Preliminaries

This section tackles two fundamental, yet under-explored questions in pseudo-supervised anomaly segmentation with synthetic abnormalities. The reasoning offers insights for designing the proposed solution.

Q1: About pseudo anomaly generation: Should pseudo-anomalies approximate the common queries in the test set?

Pseudo anomaly is introduced to establish the boundary that distinguishes abnormality, transforming the unsupervised problem into pseudo-supervision, which helps the model learn normal patterns by providing negative samples. Since there is no clear definition of what constitutes an anomaly, there shouldn't be any bound or limit on pseudo anomaly synthesis. Instead of focusing on creating pseudo anomalies that match known abnormal patterns in queries, we advocate generating a diversity of anomalies to facilitate a model to learn the comprehensive normal spectrum. In particular, when dealing with unsupervised tumor segmentation, we believe that generating a large diversity of pseudo anomalies in terms of intensity, shape, and textures facilitates addressing the high heterogeneity in tumors. This motivates the design of the proposed pseudo anomaly generation module.

Q2: About model training: Should the model training follow the exact supervised training principles on synthetic anomalies?

The success of supervised learning relies on the IID assumption that both the training and test data follow an identical distribution. Under this assumption, a model is usually well-trained on the training set with multiple iterations. However, we argue that one shouldn't follow the same philosophy to train a model on pseudo anomalies in anomaly detection and segmentation. According to the reasoning in **Q1**, a covariate shift is likely to exist between the synthesized and query anomalies. We visualize this covariate shift by 2-D TSNE in Fig. 1(C), where both tumor samples and normal images are from the LiTs dataset [3]. Consequently, due to the potential covariate shift between the synthesized and the common anomalies in pseudo-supervised segmentation, training a model on the pseudo anomalies may cause a bias and harm its performance on real queries. In another words, a good-fit model on the pseudo-anomaly data may fail on real testing data. Our ablation experiment shown in Fig. 3 validates this hypothesis. Therefore, unlike conventional supervised learning that requires a relatively long training time, we argue that model optimization on anomaly synthesis for pseudo-supervised segmentation should stop early to preserve the model's generalizability on queries. Our answer to **Q2** inspires us to design the two-phase training strategy in this study.

3   Method

Toward unsupervised liver tumor segmentation, we incorporate our reasoning to **Q1** and **Q2** into the DRAEM-similar [32] architecture. As depicted in

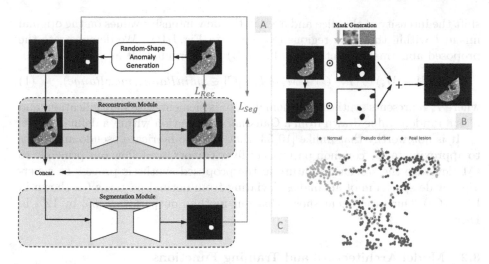

Fig. 1. (A) Systematic diagram of the proposed unsupervised liver tumor segmentation scheme. During training, synthetic abnormalities are fed to a restoration net followed by a segmentation net. To avoid model overfitting on synthesis, the two models are trained in two phases represented by blue and orange, respectively. In inference, a query is directly passed to the two networks for segmentation. (B) Proposed synthesis pipeline based on Gaussian noise stretching. (C) Liver image embedding by 2-D TSNE. (Color figure online)

Fig. 1(A), the framework comprises random-shape anomaly generation, a restoration network, and a segmentation network. Unlike DRAEM training both networks jointly, we propose a two-phase learning to avoid segmentation model over-fitting on synthetic abnormalities. In inference, only the reconstructive network and segmentation network are deployed on queries. Compared to DRAEM, our experiments show that both the proposed anomaly generation module and the two-phase learning strategy boost the liver tumor segmentation performance in terms of segmentation accuracy and model stability.

3.1 Pseudo Anomaly Generation

The anomalous training samples are simulated by the anomaly synthesis module, which generates masks of random shapes and sizes through Gaussian noise and morphological transformations. Initially, Gaussian noise is generated with the same resolution as a normal image and then blurred with a Gaussian kernel. The noise is then stretched and thresholded to produce a binarized mask. Subsequently, closing and opening operations with the elliptical kernel are applied to the binarized mask to obtain an anomaly segmentation mask. The detailed algorithm is shown in Algorithm 1 in Supplementary.

Using the generated anomaly mask M_s, we proceed to synthesize the abnormal sample I_s. In CT slides, unhealthy patterns in liver regions are demonstrated by abnormal Hounsfield-Unit (HU) values. Therefore, we propose to randomly shift the intensity of the slice and overlay the new intensity values on the original image I within the mask regions (as shown in Fig. 1(B)). We demonstrate the proposed abnormality synthesis in Fig. 1(B) and formulate it as

$$I_s = (1 - M_s) \odot (I + C) + M_s \odot I, \quad |C| \in (minRange, maxRange), \qquad (1)$$

where I_s represents synthesized anomalies, $\odot$ is element-wise multiplication, and C is a random value drawn from a Gaussian distribution within a defined range.

It is noteworthy that unlike [10,33] that aims to fabricate pseudo anomalies to approximate the common patterns of liver tumors, we follow our principle to **Q1**, leverage the stochastic nature in the proposed synthesis process to generate a wide spectrum of anomalies deviating from normal patterns (as shown in Fig. 1(C)). Our experiment shows that our method outperforms [33] by 12% in Dice.

3.2   Model Architecture and Training Functions

The reconstruction network is trained to restore anomalous regions while preserving the normal regions. The segmentation network takes the concatenation of the restoration and pseudo-anomalous image as input and targets to estimate an accurate segmentation map for the anomaly. For the reconstruction network, we use U-Net [21] with 3 encoder and decoder blocks as backbones. The specific encoder block in the restoration network adopts the architecture proposed in [11], where it consists of 2 weight-standardized convolutions [19] followed by swish activation [20] and group normalization [29].

To address diverse levels of model optimization complexity, we train the two networks consequently in two phases. The reconstruction model is first trained to restore the anomalous region in synthetic abnormal images with L_1 loss:

$$L_{rec}(I_s, \tilde{I}_s) = |I_s - \tilde{I}_s|, \qquad (2)$$

where $I_s, \tilde{I}_s$ are the pseudo outlier augmented sample and the reconstruction image. After freezing the well-trained generative module, we slightly train the segmentation model to avoid bias introduced by the covariance shift. To accommodate potential small tumors, Focal Loss [17] is adopted:

$$L_{seg}(M_s, \tilde{M}_s) = -\frac{1}{N} \sum_{i=1}^{N} \sum_{j=1}^{C} \alpha_j (1 - \tilde{m}_{s,ij})^\gamma \log(\tilde{m}_{s,ij}) \qquad (3)$$

where $\tilde{m}_{s,ij}$ is the predicted probability of class j at pixel i and α_j is the weight for class j, and $M_s, \tilde{M}_s$ are the ground truth and the estimated anomaly masks.

4   Experiments

4.1   Experimental Setting

Dataset Preparation: We evaluate the proposed method on the Liver Tumor Segmentation (LiTs) dataset [3] from MICCAI 2017 challenge. LiTs dataset consists of 131 abdominal computed tomography (CT) scans with the paired liver and liver tumour ground truth labels. Unlike with previous works [7, 16], which perform the cross-fold validation on the LiTs dataset, we argue that training on the retrieved partial samples from an unhealthy CT scan is not ideal for the model to learn the complete liver feature distribution. Therefore, we train our model on an anomaly-free dataset BTCV [14], which provides 40 healthy CT abdomen scans and the corresponding organ masks.

Table 1. Liver tumor segmentation on LiTs [3]. Our method exhibits the best Dice with a standard deviation 1.78. Results with * are directly copied from original papers.

Methods	Supervision	Dice
Zhang et al. [33]	✓	61.91*
DRAEM [32]	X	14.75
Zhang et al. [33]	X	40.78*
ASC-Net [7]	X	32.24*
ASC-Net + postprocessing [7]	X	50.23*
Hu et al. [10]	X	**59.77***
Ours	X	53.03

For all CT volumes in training and test, HU values are transformed into grayscale and the liver Region of Interest (ROI) is extracted according to the organ annotations. Then 2D slices are obtained along the Axial plane, resized to 256 × 256, and normalized independently by histogram equalization.

Implementation Details: We run the experiments on dual Nvidia RTX-3090 GPUs. The threshold for pseudo mask generation is set to be 200, and the intensity range of the random intensity shift is $[-100, 100]$. The focal loss parameters are defined as $\alpha = 1$ and $\gamma = 2$. We use PyTorch [18] to implement the proposed method. The model is trained for 200 epochs for the first stage and just 1 epoch for the second stage to avoid bias introduced by pseudo anomalies. The learning rate is set to 0.0001, with a batch size of 8 using Adam [12] optimizer. We follow previous studies and use the Dice score as our evaluation metric.

4.2 Results and Discussion

Comparison to SOTA: We quantitatively compare the proposed method with state-of-the-art unsupervised liver tumor segmentation methods including Zhang et al. [33], Hu et al. [10] ASC-Net [7] both with and without manually-designed post-processing and report the results in Table 1. The fully supervised method is taken as performance upper bound. As shown in Table 1, our approach significantly outperforms the other methods, with the exception of [10] and shrinks the gap between unsupervised method and fully-supervision. Notably, [10] leverages extensive clinical prior knowledge to synthesize pseudo anomalies resembling real tumors. Furthermore, our approach achieves a substantial reduction in runtime at $0.018\,s/slice$, compared to $0.476\,s/slice$ in [10] which operates on 3D volume, incurring higher memory usage and slower inference time. In Fig. 2, we show our segmentation results on real tumor data in the LiTs dataset.

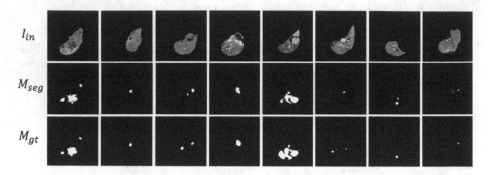

Fig. 2. Tumor segmentation on real liver tumor data, from easy (left) to difficult (right). I_{in}: Input , M_{seg}: segmentation mask, and M_{gt}: Ground-Truth.

Table 2. Ablation study of two-phase training (TP), pseudo anomaly (PA), and reconstructive network. The baseline is DRAEM model [32]. Asterisks indicate statistical significance (*: $p \le 0.05$, **: $p \le 0.001$) when using a paired Student's t-test compared to the baseline.

Method	$+TP$	$+PA$	$+U\text{-}Net$	Dice
Baseline				14.75 ± 14.28
Baseline	✓			21.31 ± 12.54
Baseline	✓	✓		$30.17 \pm 5.50^*$
Baseline		✓	✓	$40.06 \pm 6.85^*$
Baseline	✓	✓	✓	$\mathbf{53.03 \pm 1.78^{**}}$

Ablation on Model Components: The proposed method and DRAEM differ in three aspects: pseudo anomaly generation (corresponding to **Q1**), two-phase training (corresponding to **Q2**), and U-Net backbone in the restoration net. In this ablation study, we take the DRAEM as baseline, decouple these factors, and evaluate their impact in terms of tumor detection (by AUROC) and segmentation (by DICE) on LiTs. We run this ablation 3 times, and the performance is reported in Table 2. Due to page limitation, additional results such as AUROC, anomaly size mask threshold selection, and a wide spectrum of pseudo anomalous samples can be found in supplementary.

The two-phase training strategy improves Dice by 6.5% on the baseline. When combined with U-Net and PA, there's a significant 13% performance boost compared to using only U-Net and PA, validating our hypothesis that light segmentation training on pseudo anomalies helps address the covariant shift between synthetic anomalies and real tumors. We further extended the training of the segmentation net to 200 epochs and captured tumor detection performance (by AUROC) and segmentation quality (by Dice) every 5 epochs. It's worth emphasizing that these experiments incorporate the synergistic application of TA, U-Net and PA, as this combination has proven to demonstrate optimal outcomes with TA. Therefore, Fig. 3 results diverge from the Dice score in Table 2, where TA solely influences the baseline, yielding a comparatively less pronounced impact on reducing training perturbation. As shown in Fig. 3, the mean AUROC keeps decreasing, and the standard deviation keeps increasing. The perturbation also occurs in Dice after 50 epochs. We attribute this to model overfitting on the pseudo data, which hurts model's generalizability on queries.

Additionally, the proposed anomaly synthesis module and U-Net designed in our restoration net significantly boost the segmentation performance. Figure 4 presents a visualization comparison of reconstructions generated by autoencoder (AE) and U-Net. Compared to the AE-based network, the skip-connection in U-Net helps preserve the texture details in liver reconstruction images, which facilitates the downstream segmentation task.

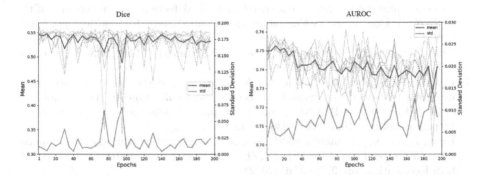

Fig. 3. An illustrative depiction of the evaluation performance of the segmentation network reveals a tendency to overfit shortly after a short period of training. Throughout this process, the reconstruction network maintains a frozen state.

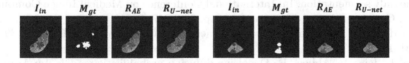

Fig. 4. Visualization of image reconstruction by AE and U-Net.

5   Conclusion

In this study, we tackled the challenging problem of unsupervised liver tumor segmentation and proposed a two-stage pseudo-supervision solution with synthetic anomalies. By generating anomalies spreading over a large spectrum, the synthesis data facilitated the model in finding normal sample boundary in embedding space. The two-stage training strategy mitigated the impact of covariant shift between synthesis data and actual tumor data on model optimization, and thus avoid segmentation model's overfitting on synthetic anomalies. Experimentation suggested that the proposed method performs comparably to SOTA methods. Looking ahead, we aspire to extend our exploration of model performance to encompass various other diseases and data modalities and investigate the integration of both real and synthetic tumor within the model training pipeline.

References

1. Akçay, S., Atapour-Abarghouei, A., Breckon, T.P.: Skip-ganomaly: skip connected and adversarially trained encoder-decoder anomaly detection. In: 2019 International Joint Conference on Neural Networks (IJCNN), pp. 1–8 (2019)
2. Bergmann, P., Fauser, M., Sattlegger, D., Steger, C.: MVTec AD-a comprehensive real-world dataset for unsupervised anomaly detection. In: Proceedings of the IEEE/CVF Conference on Computer Vision and Pattern Recognition, pp. 9592–9600 (2019)
3. Bilic, P., et al.: The liver tumor segmentation benchmark (LITS). arXiv:1901.04056 (2019)
4. Defard, T., Setkov, A., Loesch, A., Audigier, R.: PaDiM: a patch distribution modeling framework for anomaly detection and localization. In: Del Bimbo, A., et al. (eds.) ICPR 2021. LNCS, vol. 12664, pp. 475–489. Springer, Cham (2021). https://doi.org/10.1007/978-3-030-68799-1_35
5. Deng, H., Li, X.: Anomaly detection via reverse distillation from one-class embedding. In: Proceedings of the IEEE/CVF Conference on Computer Vision and Pattern Recognition, pp. 9737–9746 (2022)
6. Deng, H., Li, X.: Self-supervised anomaly detection with random-shape pseudo-outliers. In: 2022 44th Annual International Conference of the IEEE Engineering in Medicine & Biology Society (EMBC), pp. 4768–4772 (2022)
7. Dey, R., Hong, Y.: ASC-Net: adversarial-based selective network for unsupervised anomaly segmentation. In: International Conference on Medical Image Computing and Computer-Assisted Intervention, pp. 236–247 (2021)
8. Goodfellow, I.: Generative adversarial networks. Commun. ACM **63**(11), 139–144 (2020)
9. Ho, J., Jain, A., Abbeel, P.: Denoising diffusion probabilistic models. In: Advances in Neural Information Processing Systems, vol. 33, pp. 6840–6851 (2020)
10. Hu, Q., et al.: Label-free liver tumor segmentation. In: Proceedings of the IEEE/CVF Conference on Computer Vision and Pattern Recognition, pp. 7422–7432 (2023)
11. Kascenas, A., Pugeault, N., O'Neil, A.Q.: Denoising autoencoders for unsupervised anomaly detection in brain MRI. In: Medical Imaging with Deep Learning (2021)

12. Kingma, D.P., Ba, J.: Adam: a method for stochastic optimization. arXiv:1412.6980 (2014)
13. Kingma, D.P., Welling, M.: Auto-encoding variational bayes. arXiv:1312.6114 (2013)
14. Landman, B., Xu, Z., Igelsias, J., Styner, M., Langerak, T., Klein, A.: MICCAI multi-atlas labeling beyond the cranial vault-workshop and challenge. In: Proceedings of the MICCAI Multi-Atlas Labeling Beyond Cranial Vault-Workshop Challenge, vol. 5, p. 12 (2015)
15. Li, C.L., Sohn, K., Yoon, J., Pfister, T.: CutPaste: self-supervised learning for anomaly detection and localization. In: Proceedings of the IEEE/CVF Conference on Computer Vision and Pattern Recognition, pp. 9664–9674 (2021)
16. Li, H., Iwamoto, Y., Han, X., Lin, L., Hu, H., Chen, Y.W.: An accurate unsupervised liver lesion detection method using pseudo-lesions. In: Wang, L., Dou, Q., Fletcher, P.T., Speidel, S., Li, S. (eds.) MICCAI 2022. LNCS, vol. 13438, pp. 214–223. Springer, Cham (2022). https://doi.org/10.1007/978-3-031-16452-1_21
17. Lin, T.Y., Goyal, P., Girshick, R., He, K., Dollár, P.: Focal loss for dense object detection. In: Proceedings of the IEEE International Conference on Computer Vision, pp. 2980–2988 (2017)
18. Paszke, A., et al.: PyTorch: an imperative style, high-performance deep learning library. In: Advances in Neural Information Processing Systems, vol. 32, pp. 8024–8035 (2019)
19. Qiao, S., Wang, H., Liu, C., Shen, W., Yuille, A.: Micro-batch training with batch-channel normalization and weight standardization. arXiv:1903.10520 (2019)
20. Ramachandran, P., Zoph, B., Le, Q.V.: Searching for activation functions. arXiv:1710.05941 (2017)
21. Ronneberger, O., Fischer, P., Brox, T.: U-Net: convolutional networks for biomedical image segmentation. In: Navab, N., Hornegger, J., Wells, W.M., Frangi, A.F. (eds.) MICCAI 2015. LNCS, vol. 9351, pp. 234–241. Springer, Cham (2015). https://doi.org/10.1007/978-3-319-24574-4_28
22. Roth, K., Pemula, L., Zepeda, J., Schölkopf, B., Brox, T., Gehler, P.: Towards total recall in industrial anomaly detection. In: Proceedings of the IEEE/CVF Conference on Computer Vision and Pattern Recognition, pp. 14318–14328 (2022)
23. Salehi, M., Sadjadi, N., Baselizadeh, S., Rohban, M.H., Rabiee, H.R.: Multiresolution knowledge distillation for anomaly detection. In: Proceedings of the IEEE/CVF Conference on Computer Vision and Pattern Recognition, pp. 14902–14912 (2021)
24. Schlegl, T., Seeböck, P., Waldstein, S.M., Schmidt-Erfurth, U., Langs, G.: Unsupervised anomaly detection with generative adversarial networks to guide marker discovery. In: International Conference on Information Processing in Medical Imaging, pp. 146–157 (2017)
25. Tan, J., Hou, B., Batten, J., Qiu, H., Kainz, B.: Detecting outliers with foreign patch interpolation. arXiv:2011.04197 (2020)
26. Tan, J., Hou, B., Day, T., Simpson, J., Rueckert, D., Kainz, B.: Detecting outliers with poisson image interpolation. In: International Conference on Medical Image Computing and Computer-Assisted Intervention, pp. 581–591 (2021)
27. Wang, M., et al.: Unsupervised anomaly detection with local-sensitive VQVAE and global-sensitive transformers. arXiv:2303.17505 (2023)
28. Wolleb, J., Bieder, F., Sandkühler, R., Cattin, P.C.: Diffusion models for medical anomaly detection. In: International Conference on Medical Image Computing and Computer-Assisted Intervention, pp. 35–45 (2022)

29. Wu, Y., He, K.: Group normalization. In: Ferrari, V., Hebert, M., Sminchisescu, C., Weiss, Y. (eds.) ECCV 2018. LNCS, vol. 11217, pp. 3–19. Springer, Cham (2018). https://doi.org/10.1007/978-3-030-01261-8_1

30. Wyatt, J., Leach, A., Schmon, S.M., Willcocks, C.G.: AnoDDPM: anomaly detection with denoising diffusion probabilistic models using simplex noise. In: Proceedings of the IEEE/CVF Conference on Computer Vision and Pattern Recognition, pp. 650–656 (2022)

31. Yao, Q., Xiao, L., Liu, P., Zhou, S.K.: Label-free segmentation of COVID-19 lesions in lung CT. IEEE Trans. Med. Imaging 40(10), 2808–2819 (2021)

32. Zavrtanik, V., Kristan, M., Skočaj, D.: DRAEM-a discriminatively trained reconstruction embedding for surface anomaly detection. In: Proceedings of the IEEE/CVF International Conference on Computer Vision, p. 8330–8339 (2021)

33. Zhang, X., Xie, W., Huang, C., Zhang, Y., Wang, Y.: Self-supervised tumor segmentation through layer decomposition. arXiv:2109.03230 (2021)

34. Zimmerer, D., Isensee, F., Petersen, J., Kohl, S., Maier-Hein, K.: Unsupervised anomaly localization using variational auto-encoders. In: Shen, D., et al. (eds.) MICCAI 2019. LNCS, vol. 11767, pp. 289–297. Springer, Cham (2019). https://doi.org/10.1007/978-3-030-32251-9_32

Improving Style Transfer in Dynamic Contrast Enhanced MRI Using a Spatio-Temporal Approach

Adam G. Tattersall[1,2]([✉]), Keith A. Goatman[2], Lucy E. Kershaw[1],
Scott I. K. Semple[1], and Sonia Dahdouh[2]

[1] University of Edinburgh, Edinburgh, UK
adam.tattersall@ed.ac.uk
[2] Canon Medical Research Europe (CMRE), Edinburgh, UK

Abstract. Style transfer in DCE-MRI is a challenging task due to large variations in contrast enhancements across different tissues and time. Current unsupervised methods fail due to the wide variety of contrast enhancement and motion between the images in the series. We propose a new method that combines autoencoders to disentangle content and style with convolutional LSTMs to model predicted latent spaces along time and adaptive convolutions to tackle the localised nature of contrast enhancement. To evaluate our method, we propose a new metric that takes into account the contrast enhancement. Qualitative and quantitative analyses show that the proposed method outperforms the state of the art on two different datasets.

Keywords: Style Transfer · Spatio-temporal Information · Content/Style Disentanglement · Dynamic Contrast Enhanced Magnetic Resonance Imaging (DCE-MRI)

1 Introduction

DCE-MRI is a type of quantitative imaging that can be used to monitor microvascular perfusion [7]. Multiple T1 weighted images are taken rapidly over a few minutes whilst a contrast agent injection causes a rapid increase in signal intensity in tissues of interest. The resulting data contain motion and tissue-dependent contrast enhancement (CE) which makes obtaining manually annotated ground truth time consuming and difficult. Fully annotated datasets are therefore scarce, which reduces the diversity of available data to train deep learning models. We previously found that to train a robust model with DCE-MRI data, using images strategically from the whole sequence with varying contrast levels led to better performing models [16]. However, in practice this can be difficult for tasks such as segmentation when ground truth is limited. Although common augmentation techniques allow for an increase in the number of images, they do not help to synthesise new annotated examples with varying CE. A

J. M. Wolterink et al. (Eds.): SASHIMI 2023, LNCS 14288, pp. 97–106, 2023.
https://doi.org/10.1007/978-3-031-44689-4_10

method that can synthesise new images from previously annotated data would provide models with diverse examples.

In this work, we propose a new style transfer method to augment DCE-MRI with different contrast enhancement levels. Our method uses convolutional long short-term memory (LSTM) [2] networks which leverage the temporal information from DCE-MRI to better predict structures of the content image and generate images with the noise characteristics of MRI whilst allowing addition or removal of contrast enhancement. We also propose a new metric, contrast weighted (CW)- structural similarity index measure (SSIM), that uses information on the localised aspect of tissue enhancement to evaluate either structural or style similarity between a generated and a content or style image, respectively.

2   Related Work

Using neural networks for style transfer was first proposed by Gatys *et al.* [4] which used a pre-trained VGG-Network [15]. Instead of training, an iterative process of passing the content, style and output image through a pre-trained network was used. Building on this success, improvements were made to speed up the iterative process by using a feed-forward network [17] as well as creating perceptual losses [9] to give more visually pleasing results. However, these networks struggled to adapt to new styles that were introduced during inference as the network was usually tied to a small number of style images. In 2017, Huang *et al.* [5] proposed Adaptive Instance Normalisation (AdaIN) which aligns the mean and variance of the content features with those of the style features allowing for style transfer without the restriction of a pre-defined set of styles.

Successful style transfer methods have since been proposed such as learning mappings between pairs of images (Pix2Pix [8] and CycleGAN [18]) as well as content/style disentanglement methods such as Multimodal Unsupervised Image-to-Image Translation (MUNIT) [6]. Pix2Pix was able to generate high quality images using a conditional GAN but required paired and registered images to train effectively. Instead, CycleGAN can be trained using unpaired data by using two generators to map between each domain. However, both Pix2Pix and CycleGAN struggle to generate diverse outputs when new style images are introduced at inference due to learning to map between domains directly.

MUNIT offers an alternative approach using content/style disentanglement to take input images and predict latent spaces for style and content encoding. This allows style transfer whilst preserving the content of the image, giving better control for the translation process. However, MUNIT often requires a large amount of data to train as well as having large computational and memory requirements. AdaIN is also used to combine the style and content latent spaces. It can, however, result in global rather than tissue dependent enhancement which leads to the generation of unrealistic images. Additionally, MUNIT does not utilise any temporal information available in the DCE-MRI sequence.

DRIT++ [11], an extension to MUNIT, enhances diversity by introducing disentanglement at the domain level, and improving attribute manipulation.

However, it also comes with increased computational complexity, complexity in hyperparameter tuning, and a potential trade-off between diversity and fidelity.

Early work on style transfer for videos naively processed frames independently leading to flickering and false discontinuities [3]. Methods have since been proposed to ensure temporal consistency between image frames [3]. They use three components: a style sub-network, a flow sub-network and a mask sub-network. The style sub-network is an auto-encoder which performs the style transfer. The flow sub-network estimates the correspondence between consecutive image frames and warps the features. Finally, the mask sub-network regresses a mask to compose features adjacent in time, allowing for warped features to be reused. This allows for a smooth style transfer between image frames, but it is prone to errors when there is large motion between frames as well as propagating errors over time leading to inconsistent style transfer and blurriness.

3   Materials and Methods

3.1   Data

Two datasets were used. The first contains 2D kidney DCE-MRI [13] from 13 patients with 375 images acquired continuously at a temporal resolution of 1.6 s, a spatial resolution of 384×348 with pixel sizes 1.08×1.08 mm. The second contains 3D prostate DCE-MRI [12] from 20 patients with 40 volumes acquired continuously at a temporal resolution of 6 s, a spatial resolution of $256 \times 192 \times 16$ with voxel sizes $1.12 \times 1.12 \times 3.5$ mm. Each dataset was split at a patient level with an 80:20 ratio, training was done using five-fold cross validation.

3.2   Global Architecture

Inspired by MUNIT, we use a structure composed of encoders and decoders to first disentangle content and style latent spaces and recombine them to generate new images. Successful disentanglement should lead to content latent spaces containing information representing the structures of the image and style latent spaces containing information representing the modality (MRI) and contrast enhancements. However, temporal information is not taken into account in most style transfer methods. Within DCE-MRI, information such as structures within organs become visible when there are various levels of contrast enhancement at different time points. In our method, we use additional content encoders to predict latent spaces for images from multiple time points. Then, we pass the predicted content latent spaces to a convolutional LSTM [2] which has been set up to be bi-directional. We use a convolutional LSTM as this allows modelling of the temporal information from a sequence of images. It leverages spatial invariance by extracting relevant features from the images regardless of their position. Using a bi-directional LSTM allows better contextual understanding of the time series data by accessing past and future events. This allows content visible at

various time points to be learnt. The overall architecture is shown in Fig. 1. At inference the images are passed through the encoders and decoders once to perform style transfer.

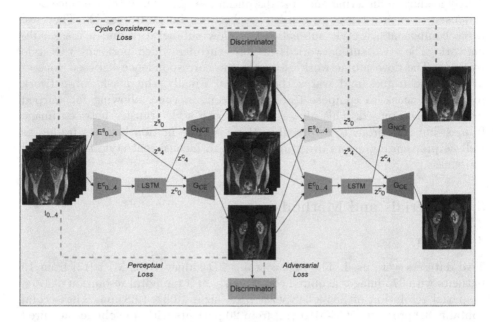

Fig. 1. Our model takes an input I of 5 images/volumes to content encoders $E^c_{0...4}$ and style encoders $E^s_{0...4}$. Generators G_{CE} and G_{NCE} construct images from latent spaces z predicted by the content and style encoders. We also show the losses used: cycle consistency, perceptual and adversarial. For clarity of the figure, we have only shown one example for each of the losses.

3.3 Instance Normalisation

AdaIN [5] is used to normalise the activations in a neural network based on the statistics of the style image. This enables the transfer of style from the style image to the content image by matching their statistical properties. However, by only using global style information, contrast enhancement is performed on the whole image instead of specific tissues. To overcome this, we use AdaConv [1] which captures global and local information to predict parameters to combine style and content latent spaces. Three convolutional neural networks are used to predict a depth-wise spatial kernel, a point-wise kernel and a bias. The kernels and bias are then convolved with the content code.

3.4 Losses

The L1 loss between the original and reconstructed images and between the initially predicted and reconstructed latent spaces is used to ensure that important

information such as structure is not lost during the reconstruction and translation process. Furthermore, the L1 loss is known for its smooth gradients which can facilitate stable and effective optimisation during the training process. A mean squared error (MSE) loss is also used as an adversarial loss to help generate images that are indistinguishable from the real images.

While those two losses were used in MUNIT, we found that some important textural characteristics of the images were lost in the generated images. To improve this, we also used two additional perceptual loss functions proposed by Johnson *et al.* [9] for style transfer and super resolution tasks. The first is a feature reconstruction loss which is the squared, normalised Euclidean distance (Eq. 1). This encourages the feature representations predicted by a pretrained model P of the content image x and the generated image g to be similar. f is the dimension of the feature map.

$$L_{feature} = \frac{1}{f}||P(g) - P(x)||_2^2 \qquad (1)$$

Next, we use a style reconstruction loss to penalise differences in style between the style image y and the generated image g. This loss uses the squared Frobenius norm of the difference between the Gram matrices of the feature representations predicted by a pretrained network P (Eq. 2). Minimising this loss encourages the generated image to capture style patterns and textures that are similar to the style image. The Frobenius norm is a measure of the magnitude of the matrix, and using it as the loss term allows the model to focus on preserving the overall style content and structure.

$$L_{Frob} = ||Gram(P(g)) - Gram(P(y))||_F^2 \qquad (2)$$

For the 2D data, we used a VGG-16 pre-trained network on ImageNet [14] converted to grayscale. For the 3D data we used MedicalNet which is a pretrained multi-modal multi-tissue ResNet-18 backbone.

3.5   Evaluating Style Transfer

Quantitatively evaluating style transfer is difficult with unpaired, unregistered data. Metrics such as peak signal to noise ratio (PSNR), SSIM and multiscale (MS)-SSIM primarily focus on the pixel-level similarity between a pair of images. This makes it difficult to evaluate style transfer in DCE-MRI due to the large variety of CE in an image and the localised aspect of it. We propose a contrast weighted (CW)-SSIM (Eq. 3) as a metric to measure both the content structure as well as evaluate the amount of CE (addition or removal) in the style image.

For evaluating content, we weight the SSIM with a distance map *dist_map* created by calculating the shortest distance from each voxel to a contrast enhanced voxel. The distances were normalised between 0.1 and 1. We determined which voxels were contrast enhanced by subtracting each image from the first non-CE image and calculated the average. Then, we used an empirical threshold of 20 to determine which voxels were contrast enhanced. To evaluate style, we inverted the distance map so that a voxel has a higher weighting when it is closer to a contrast enhanced voxel. x is the generated image and y is either the content or style image.

$$CW\text{-}SSIM(x, y, dist\_map) = SSIM(x \cdot dist\_map, y \cdot dist\_map) \qquad (3)$$

3.6 Implementation

We used PyTorch and trained with the Adam optimiser, a learning rate of 0.001 and batch size of 8 for 2D and 5 for 3D. Early stopping was used with a patience of 20. Our experiments were run on an RTX Titan GPU. We compared our method with MUNIT, CycleGAN and StyleGAN3 [10]. DRIT++ was not used due to the large computational requirements with 3D data.

4 Results

Tables 1 and 2 show our quantitative results: PSNR between the style (image we want to transfer style from) and generated image, SSIM and MS-SSIM between the content (image we want to take structure from) and generated image and finally, our proposed weighted SSIMs. For each style transfer direction and metric, our method consistently outperforms the other approaches. Figures 2 and 3 qualitatively highlight the good results of our method on 2D and 3D datasets. In addition, quantitative results on both figures show that our proposed metric preserves qualitative ordering of results for both style and content. In comparison, metrics such as SSIM struggle to accurately correlate to visual results.

5 Discussion

In this work, we proposed a method for style transfer that leverages spatio-temporal information, applied to DCE-MRI. Using convolutional LSTMs we are

Table 1. Quantitative results for each approach when adding or removing CE in the kidney. The mean and standard deviation is shown for each metric.

Metric	Direction	MUNIT	CycleGAN	StyleGAN3	Our Method
PSNR	Non-CE to CE	70.6 ± 3.2	66.5 ± 2.7	52.3 ± 3.9	**81.3 ± 2.7**
	CE to Non-CE	71.5 ± 3.4	66.8 ± 2.8	51.9 ± 3.8	**78.5 ± 2.6**
SSIM	Non-CE to CE	0.61 ± 0.05	0.66 ± 0.06	0.32 ± 0.06	**0.89 ± 0.04**
	CE to Non-CE	0.58 ± 0.04	0.58 ± 0.05	0.34 ± 0.07	**0.88 ± 0.03**
MS-SSIM	Non-CE to CE	0.55 ± 0.04	0.43 ± 0.07	0.34 ± 0.04	**0.82 ± 0.03**
	CE to Non-CE	0.52 ± 0.04	0.45 ± 0.05	0.37 ± 0.05	**0.79 ± 0.04**
Content **CW-SSIM**	Non-CE to CE	0.73 ± 0.03	0.61 ± 0.05	0.47 ± 0.05	**0.95 ± 0.02**
	CE to Non-CE	0.69 ± 0.03	0.57 ± 0.05	0.41 ± 0.05	**0.94 ± 0.02**
Style **CW-SSIM**	Non-CE to CE	0.64 ± 0.03	0.41 ± 0.05	0.67 ± 0.05	**0.74 ± 0.02**
	CE to Non-CE	0.62 ± 0.03	0.49 ± 0.05	0.64 ± 0.05	**0.72 ± 0.02**

able to model changes in structures caused by CE across the temporal dimension giving better content latent spaces. In addition, using localised style information instead of a global one by making use of AdaConv helped to tackle the local nature of CE in DCE-MRI.

Qualitative evaluation shows that the proposed method leads to sharper images, better content preservation, better localised CE and realistic MRI appearance. Quantitatively, we outperform the other algorithms with each met-

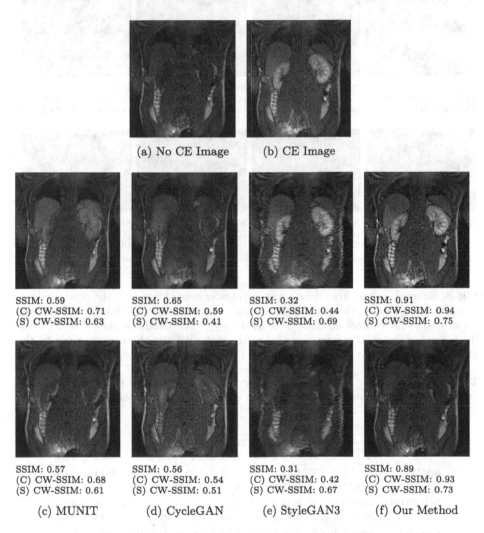

(a) No CE Image   (b) CE Image

SSIM: 0.59   SSIM: 0.65   SSIM: 0.32   SSIM: 0.91
(C) CW-SSIM: 0.71   (C) CW-SSIM: 0.59   (C) CW-SSIM: 0.44   (C) CW-SSIM: 0.94
(S) CW-SSIM: 0.63   (S) CW-SSIM: 0.41   (S) CW-SSIM: 0.69   (S) CW-SSIM: 0.75

SSIM: 0.57   SSIM: 0.56   SSIM: 0.31   SSIM: 0.89
(C) CW-SSIM: 0.68   (C) CW-SSIM: 0.54   (C) CW-SSIM: 0.42   (C) CW-SSIM: 0.93
(S) CW-SSIM: 0.61   (S) CW-SSIM: 0.51   (S) CW-SSIM: 0.67   (S) CW-SSIM: 0.73

(c) MUNIT   (d) CycleGAN   (e) StyleGAN3   (f) Our Method

Fig. 2. Example results from different style transfer approaches with the kidney data. The first row (a and b) shows the input images. The second row shows the results when (a) is used as the content image and (b) as the style. The third row shows results when (b) is used as the content image and (a) as the style. We also show scores given by the SSIM, content (C) CW-SSIM and style (S) CW-SSIM.

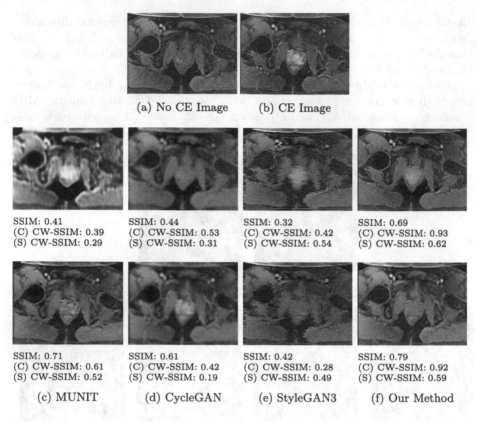

(a) No CE Image   (b) CE Image

SSIM: 0.41
(C) CW-SSIM: 0.39
(S) CW-SSIM: 0.29

SSIM: 0.44
(C) CW-SSIM: 0.53
(S) CW-SSIM: 0.31

SSIM: 0.32
(C) CW-SSIM: 0.42
(S) CW-SSIM: 0.54

SSIM: 0.69
(C) CW-SSIM: 0.93
(S) CW-SSIM: 0.62

SSIM: 0.71
(C) CW-SSIM: 0.61
(S) CW-SSIM: 0.52

SSIM: 0.61
(C) CW-SSIM: 0.42
(S) CW-SSIM: 0.19

SSIM: 0.42
(C) CW-SSIM: 0.28
(S) CW-SSIM: 0.49

SSIM: 0.79
(C) CW-SSIM: 0.92
(S) CW-SSIM: 0.59

(c) MUNIT   (d) CycleGAN   (e) StyleGAN3   (f) Our Method

Fig. 3. Example results from different style transfer approaches with the prostate data. The first row (a and b) shows the input images. The second row shows the results when (a) is used as the content image and (b) as the style. The third row shows results when (b) is used as the content image and (a) as the style. We also show scores given by the SSIM, content (C) CW-SSIM and style (S) CW-SSIM.

Table 2. Quantitative results for each approach when adding or removing CE in the prostate. The mean and standard deviation is shown for each metric.

Metric	Direction	MUNIT	CycleGAN	StyleGAN3	Our Method
PSNR	Non-CE to CE	40.6 ± 4.3	52.2 ± 3.8	43.5 ± 5.2	**72.1 ± 3.6**
	CE to Non-CE	68.7 ± 4.1	61.2 ± 3.4	51.9 ± 6.1	**68.9 ± 4.1**
SSIM	Non-CE to CE	0.41 ± 0.06	0.46 ± 0.05	0.36 ± 0.09	**0.71 ± 0.04**
	CE to Non-CE	0.69 ± 0.04	0.59 ± 0.05	0.43 ± 0.08	**0.78 ± 0.03**
MS-SSIM	Non-CE to CE	0.49 ± 0.04	0.38 ± 0.06	0.28 ± 0.05	**0.76 ± 0.04**
	CE to Non-CE	0.47 ± 0.04	0.39 ± 0.05	0.32 ± 0.06	**0.71 ± 0.03**
Content	Non-CE to CE	0.38 ± 0.04	0.52 ± 0.05	0.41 ± 0.05	**0.92 ± 0.03**
CW-SSIM	CE to Non-CE	0.63 ± 0.04	0.46 ± 0.04	0.32 ± 0.06	**0.93 ± 0.04**
Style	Non-CE to CE	0.34 ± 0.05	0.28 ± 0.06	0.52 ± 0.07	**0.59 ± 0.05**
CW-SSIM	CE to Non-CE	0.53 ± 0.04	0.21 ± 0.05	0.47 ± 0.06	**0.57 ± 0.04**

ric, for each style transfer direction. While we expected that adding CE to images would be an easier task than removing CE, we found that for both tasks the method exhibits similarly performing quantitative and qualitative results. The results for style transfer with the kidney data show that when there is clear CE, it is easier to perform style transfer in both directions. However, when style transfer is performed on the prostate data, the model struggles in comparison to the kidney data. This may be due to the enhancement of the prostate being less defined than the kidney data. In Fig. 3b, we can see the prostate with CE. Compared to Fig. 2b showing kidneys with CE, it is harder to determine the edges. The two original images shown in Figs. 3a and 3b are clear and easy to see some edges of prostate, in other images, it is harder to see the edges of the prostate.

Our metric, CW-SSIM, enables the evaluation of the quality of the content and style of the generated images when there are large differences in CE. When comparing against the qualitative results, the quality of the style transfer is in line with each of the CW-SSIM results. By using two weightings: areas of CE and without CE, we are able to evaluate the similarity between structures where intensity differences are small to measure for content similarity. By using an inverted map, we can also compare regions of high CE to measure the differences in style between the generated and style image. An advantage of this metric over SSIM or MS-SSIM is that we are able to separate the evaluation of content and style to ensure that key structures in the image remain, whilst changing the intensity values to match the style. This is important with DCE-MRI as large intensity changes are localised in specific tissues. When we compare the results for the prostate using MS-SSIM and style CW-SSIM, we can see that the style CW-SSIM gave a much lower score. This follows the qualitative results closely as the styles of each of the generated images are not similar to the style image used. By evaluating the areas of the image separately we remove the possibility of parts of the image with little CE inflating the score given by the SSIM.

A limitation to our style transfer approach is that better style transfer was achieved with the kidney data compared to the prostate data. This may be due to the structures in the prostate data not being as clearly defined as the kidney data, as well as the prostate not enhancing as clearly as the kidney. Similarly to MUNIT, our method has large computational and memory requirements. Using our method, new images can be generated, to contain a variety of stages of CE. This type of augmentation allows a small number of images to be manually annotated making it easier to train robust models for image processing tasks.

6   Conclusion

We proposed a style transfer method which used temporal information with disentangled representations. Our method learns information from time series data and accurately captures key structures from content images whilst localising the addition of CE. Our method is trained in an unsupervised setting with unpaired data. Qualitative and quantitative analysis shows that our method outperforms other popular style transfer techniques. We also proposed a new metric which uses information based on the localised aspect of tissue enhancement with contrast in DCE-MRI to evaluate similarity to the style or content image.

Acknowledgements. This work was funded by Medical Research Scotland and CMRE.

References

1. Chandran, P., Zoss, G., Gotardo, P., Gross, M., Bradley, D.: Adaptive Convolutions for Structure-Aware Style Transfer. CVPR (2021)
2. Chao, Z., Pu, F., Yin, Y., Han, B., Chen, X.: Research on real-time local rainfall prediction based on MEMS sensors. J. Sens. (2018)
3. Chen, D., Liao, J., Yuan, L., Yu, N., Hua, G.: Coherent online video style transfer. In: IEEE ICCV (2017)
4. Gatys, L., Ecker, A., Bethge, M.: A neural algorithm of artistic style. J. Vis. (2016)
5. Huang, X., Belongie, S.: Arbitrary style transfer in real-time with adaptive instance normalization. IEEE ICCV (2017)
6. Huang, X., Liu, M.Y., Belongie, S., Kautz, J.: Multimodal unsupervised image-to-image translation. In: ECCV (2018)
7. Ingrisch, M., Sourbron, S.: Tracer-kinetic modeling of dynamic contrast-enhanced MRI and CT: a primer. J. Pharmacokinetics Pharmacodyn. (2013)
8. Isola, P., Zhu, J.Y., Zhou, T., Efros, A.A.: Image-to-image translation with conditional adversarial networks. In: CVPR (2017)
9. Johnson, J., Alahi, A., Fei-Fei, L.: Perceptual losses for real-time style transfer and super-resolution. In: ECCV (2016)
10. Karras, T., et al.: Alias-free generative adversarial networks. In: NeurIPS (2021)
11. Lee, H.Y., et al.: DRIT++: diverse image-to-image translation via disentangled representations. Int. J. Comput. Vis. (2020)
12. Lemaître, G., Martí, R., Freixenet, J., Vilanova, J.C., Walker, P.M., Meriaudeau, F.: Computer-aided detection and diagnosis for prostate cancer based on mono and multi-parametric MRI: a review. Comput. Biol. Med. (2015)
13. Lietzmann, F., Zllner, F.G., Attenberger, U.I., Haneder, S., Michaely, H.J., Schad, L.R.: DCE-MRI of the human kidney using blade: a feasibility study in healthy volunteers. J. Magn. Reson. Imaging (2012)
14. Russakovsky, O., et al.: ImageNet large scale visual recognition challenge. In: IJCV (2015)
15. Simonyan, K., Zisserman, A.: Very deep convolutional networks for large-scale image recognition. In: ICLR (2015)
16. Tattersall, A.G., Goatman, K.A., Kershaw, L.E., Semple, S.I.K., Dahdouh, S.: Can a single image processing algorithm work equally well across all phases of DCE-MRI. SPIE (2023)
17. Ulyanov, D., Lebedev, V., Vedaldi, A., Lempitsky, V.: Texture networks: feed-forward synthesis of textures and stylized images. In: ICML (2016)
18. Zhu, J.Y., et al.: Toward multimodal image-to-image translation. In: NeurIPS (2017)

Synthetic Singleplex-Image Generation in Multiplex-Brightfield Immunohistochemistry Digital Pathology Using Deep Generative Models

Auranuch Lorsakul[1]([envelope]) [ORCID], Jim Martin[1], Terry Landowski[2], Erika Walker[2], Mike Flores[3], June Clements[3], Matthew Olson[3], and Gianni Ferreri[2]

[1] Computational Science and Informatics, Roche Diagnostics Solutions, Santa Clara, CA, USA
auranuch.lorsakul@roche.com
[2] Assay Development, Roche Diagnostics Solutions, Tucson, AZ, USA
[3] Clinical Development Pathology Office, Roche Diagnostics Solutions, Tucson, AZ, USA

Abstract. Multiplex-brightfield immunohistochemistry imaging (MPx) enables quantification of various biomarkers in tissue while retaining morphological and spatial information. One of the critical challenges of MPx is the complexity of visually inspection-based assessment of multiple stain intensities when they are co-localized in a cell. Consequently, it requires digital unmixing methods to separate multiple staining components and remix individual staining elements together with counterstain to become synthetic singleplex images (SPx). Unmixing MPx images becomes even more challenging when more than three biomarkers co-localized. Conventional unmixing methods e.g.,color-deconvolution or Nonnegative-Matrix-Factorization are limited and error prone when separating staining intensities of co-localized biomarkers in membrane or nuclear-subcellular compartments. Here, we exploit advances in generative-adversarial networks (GANs) based on unpaired image-to-image translation (CycleGAN) to generate synthetic SPx from MPx for pathologists to read and score. Three tonsil tissues with a total of 36 wholeslide images, stained with CD3, Bcl2, and CD8 using chromogenic detection, were used for training and evaluating our framework. Adjacent SPx were used to evaluate the visual quality of our synthetic SPx images with the following experiments: 1) performed perceptual studies or "real-vs.-fake" based on Amazon-Mechanical Turk (AMT) with pathologist observers, where results showed synthetic SPx were indistinguishable from real-adjacent SPx; and 2) evaluated whether our synthetic SPx were realistic to be scored for intensity. Results showed similarity scores of 0.96, 0.96, and 0.97 overall intensity for each synthetic SPx, respectively. Our framework provides alternative methods to virtually unmix the stains in order to accurately and efficiently generate synthetic SPx images from MPx tissue slides. This can bring confidence and opportunities for MPx *in-vitro* diagnostics.

Keywords: digital pathology · image generation · synthetic images · multiplex imaging · IHC · unmixing · cycleGAN · GAN · deep learning

J. M. Wolterink et al. (Eds.): SASHIMI 2023, LNCS 14288, pp. 107–117, 2023.
https://doi.org/10.1007/978-3-031-44689-4_11

1 Introduction

1.1 Problem Statements and Limitations

When it comes to healthcare, numerous complexities and barriers play a role in individuals receiving adequate testing and treatment. Recently, the COVID-19 pandemic has underscored the need for services and diagnostics, including deeper understanding of immunology and tumors. Multiplex assays for pathology offer a dramatic step forward in care options for patients. Combined with digital pathology, it can reach even those with otherwise limited access to healthcare.

Multiplex Immunohistochemistry (MPx). MPx technologies allow the simultaneous detection of multiple markers on a single tissue section. While MPx has been leveraged mainly in the research setting, it is being increasingly adopted in both the translational and clinical settings in response to increasing demand for improved techniques and decreased tissue availability. A number of highly multiplexed tissue imaging technologies have also emerged, permitting comprehensive studies of cell composition, functional state and cell-cell interactions which suggest improved diagnostic benefit. Quantitative image analysis can also be used to generate high-content data through application of multiplexing, which allows co-expression and co-localization analysis of multiple markers *in situ* with respect to the complex spatial context of tissue regions, including the stroma, tumor parenchyma, and invasive margin [1, 2].

Critical Challenges. One of the critical challenges of MPx is the complexity of visually inspection-based assessment of multiple stains when they are co-localized in a cell. The blending of the various stain colors, corresponding to biomarker locations, limits pathologists' diagnosis on stained MPx samples. Most recently, the development of image-analysis tools, specifically color unmixing of overlapping staining intensities, is the primary approach to support pathologists to score different biomarker expressions and delivery of diagnostic interpretations. Nevertheless, to unmix MPx images is challenging especially when there are multiple biomarkers co-localized e.g., more than two or three biomarkers. For instance, in breast cancer, the MPx assay of Estrogen Receptor (ER), Progesterone Receptor (PR), and Human Epidermal growth factor Receptor 2 (HER2) or ER-PR-HER2 with nuclear staining or hematoxylin (HTX) counterstain consists of three co-localized biomarkers for nuclear-staining patterns of biomarker ER, PR, and HTX [3].

Limitations of Current Technologies. The conventional unmixing methods such as color deconvolution [4] or Nonnegative Matrix Factorization (NMF) [5] remain limited and error prone in separating staining intensities of co-localized biomarkers in membrane or nuclear subcellular compartments. When overlapping staining intensities are used to label biomolecules such as proteins for multicolor biomarker imaging, it may become difficult to distinguish real signals from false positive signals due to bleed-through. Thus, techniques to accurately and efficiently separate signals from each biomarker become indispensable. The signal in each channel is modeled as a linear combination of the contributing staining intensities. By employing a mixing matrix, linear unmixing can produce an unmixed image. The major drawback with the linear unmixing approach is that a reference of pure stains is needed. For example, in a multiplexed brightfield panel with two or three protein biomarkers, there are overlapping emission intensities. To quantify the signal unique to each biomarker, we can utilize a reference, which could be a region of the tissue section of interest with 'pure' biomarker intensities. However, this can be problematic in highly heterogeneous tissues such as breast, colon, lung, brain, etc. Hence, challenges still remain with this approach making higher-level multiplexing difficult.

1.2 Proposed Solutions

In this study, we exploit recent advances in deep-learning image-based generation to transform MPx images to realistic synthetic singleplex (SPx) images (or virtually unmixing) that can be easily interpreted by pathologists to deliver diagnosis, semi-quantitative or qualitative assessment of protein expression, and classification of disease. Our solution performed substantially better than linear unmixing and other previous unmixing approaches. Using our framework, generating synthetic SPx images are much closer to the ground-truth SPx images created on adjacent sections. This allows robust interpretation of overlapping proteins in a cell and resolves stain-color bleed-through issues.

2 Related Work

2.1 Generative adversarial networks (GANs) in Digital Pathology

GANs have been accepted as powerful models in numerous fields including medical image analysis, computer vision, speech and language processing, etc. Recently, GANs are gaining prominence among the researchers with developments in digital pathology in several areas, such as stain normalization, tumor segmentation, and virtual staining, yet in MPx imaging.

Stain Normalization.   Bouteldja et al. [6] proposed CycleGAN to generate stain augmentation to tackle inter- and intra- stain variability existing in multi-centric cohorts of kidney pathology. This unpaired image-to-image translation approach was used as stain normalization to improve stain variability using the augmented data.

Image Segmentation.   Kapil et al. [7] introduced an end-to-end trainable network leveraging unpaired image-to-image translation between CK and PD-L1. They used GANs to jointly segment tumor epithelium on PD-L1 and extended the method to differentiate between PD-L1 positive and negative tumor epithelium regions enables the automated estimation of the PD-L1 tumor cell score. As a result, it completely bypassed the need for serial sections or re-staining of slides. Gadermayr et al. [8] proposed to generate simulated label data and perform image-to-image translation between the image and the label domain using an adversarial model. Specifically, they evaluated the segmentation of the glomeruli, an application scenario from renal pathology. They showed good results of the impact of the annotation model's accuracy as well as the effect of simulating additional low-level image features.

Virtual Staining. Gupta et al. [9] applied a GAN-based image-to-image translation approach to generate corresponding virtual stain images. The virtual samples are then merged with the original sample to create a multi-channel image, which serves as the enriched image. They applied the segmentation network on kidney pathology and obtained segmentation scores exhibiting an improvement compared to conventional processing of the original images only. With respect to the related work, image generation for MPx using the CycleGAN approach has not yet been explored in digital pathology.

3 Methodology

3.1 Proposed Framework

Advantage. One of the advantages of our framework is that it does not require paired training samples of MPx vs. SPx images, which are usually unavailable in pathological imaging. Unlike other GANs architectures (e.g., Pix2Pix [10]), a major concern is the requirement of paired images of source and target domain derived from the same location, which is not always possible in the case of real-world applications. Similarly, the paired MPx vs. SPx images are often unavailable because formalin-fixed paraffin-embedded (FFPE) slides of a tissue block were cut and stained to several slides. Consequently, these adjacent tissue slides always contain some level of tissue heterogeneity. In practice, tissues can often be several cuts away from one another, with greater levels of heterogeneity. All of these factors contribute to variability. Our unpaired image-to-image translation approach resolves this issue as it can learn to generate synthetic SPx images using unmatched sample images.

Unpaired Image-to-Image Translation (CycleGAN). This proposed approach trains a deep convolutional neural network for image-to-image translation tasks. As shown in Fig. 1, the model architecture is comprised of two pairs of generator and discriminator models. The network learns the mapping between an input (X) and an output image (Y) using a training set of unpaired images. The model contains two mapping functions $G_X:X \rightarrow Y$ and $G_Y:Y \rightarrow X$, and associated adversarial discriminators D_Y and D_X. The goal is to learn a mapping $G_X:X \rightarrow Y$ such that the distribution of images from $G_X(X)$ is indistinguishable from the distribution Y using an adversarial loss. An inverse mapping $G_Y:Y \rightarrow X$ is included as an additional constraint, introducing a cycle consistency loss [11].

The Loss and Objective Functions. For the CycleGAN objective function, there are two components consisting of an adversarial loss and a cycle consistency loss.

- *Adversarial Loss:* As illustrated in Eqs. (1) and (2), the Adversarial Loss is applied to both generators, where the generator aims to generate the images of the other domain, whereas its corresponding discriminator distinguishes between the translated samples and real samples. The generator's purpose is to minimize this loss against its corresponding discriminator that attempts to maximize it.

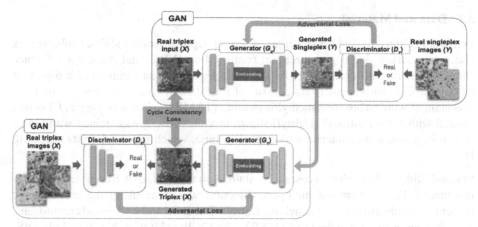

Fig. 1. The model architecture is comprised of two pairs of generator and discriminator models to map the distribution of images in the first domain (i.e., MPx) to the second domain (i.e., SPx), which are indistinguishable from the target distribution using an adversarial loss and constrained with a cycle consistency loss.

$$Loss_{adv}(G_X, D_Y, X) = \frac{1}{m} \sum_{i=1}^{m} (1 - D_Y G_X(x_i)))^2 \qquad (1)$$

$$Loss_{adv}(G_Y, D_x, Y) = \frac{1}{m} \sum_{i=1}^{m} (1 - D_X(G_Y(y_i)))^2 \qquad (2)$$

- Cycle Consistency Loss: The principal is to translate the image from one domain to the other and back as a cycle. Hence, the L_1 loss between the original image and the final generated image is calculated and the goal is to obtain the generated image that looks similar to the original image. The cycle consistency loss achieves that $G_Y(G_X(x)) \approx x$ and $G_X(G_Y(y)) \approx y$, as shown in Eq. (3).

$$Loss_{cyc}(G_X, G_Y, X, Y) = \frac{1}{m} \sum_{i=1}^{m} [G_Y(G_X(x_i)) - x_i] + \left[G_X(G_Y(y_i)) - y_i\right] \qquad (3)$$

- *Identity Loss:* The generator is enforced to preserve the color composition between the input and output domains. To pursue this, the generator is provided an image of its target domain as an input and calculating the L_1 loss between input and the generated images.

Finally, the objective function can be formed by the given loss terms, and the cycle consistency loss is weighted by a hyperparameter λ, as illustrated in Eq. (4).

$$Loss_{full} = Loss_{adv} + \lambda Loss_{cyc} \qquad (4)$$

3.2 Data and Materials

In this study, three patient subject cases including triplicate triplex slides, triplicate SPx slides per marker, one negative reagent control slide (NRC) and one-color reference slides per marker in tonsil tissue. As shown in Fig. 2(A), an example of a triplex of CD3-Bcl2-CD8 with counterstain consists of four district colors. For each color, CD3 was stained with carboxytetramethylrhodamine (TAMRA) shown in purple, CD8 was stained with benzensulfonyl (Dabsyl) shown in yellow, Bcl2 was stained with Green shown in green, and counterstain biomarker in blue, which was nuclear staining with HTX.

Stained Slides. The selected cases were stained on a VENTANA BenchMark ULTRA instrument. Fully automated multiplex detection was done using the chromogenic reagents 4-(4-dimethylaminophenylazo) Dabsyl, TAMRA, and Cy5-based chromogens, available commercially in the DISCOVERY RUO Yellow kit (Cat. No. 760–239), DIS-COVERY RUO Purple kit (Cat. No. 760–229), and DISCOVERY RUO Green HRP kit (Cat# 760–271), respectively. Staining of each biomarker was performed in sequential steps that included incubation with primary antibody and 37 °C followed by secondary anti-species antibody conjugated to either peroxidase or alkaline phosphatase. Heat denaturation at 100 °C for 8 min in ULTA Cell Conditioning 2 (CC2) was used to deactivate the antibody complex between staining cycles. Hematoxylin II and Bluing were used for counterstain [12]. Established staining protocols and test slides were evaluated by pathologists or qualified readers to ensure that background, overall staining intensity and percent coverage were concordant with each condition. Comments were also captured. These three biomarkers are expressed in a subset of lymphocytes, with CD3 and CD8 co-localized to the plasma membrane, while Bcl-2 is localized to the mitochondrial membrane in the cytoplasm. Due to the size and compact cytoplasm of tonsillar T cells, markers can appear fully co-localized, and it is possible to have a maximum of three staining colors at the overlapping location.

Scanned Slides. The stained slides were scanned at 20x magnification on a VENTANA DP200 scanner and were annotated with 10 fields of view (FOV) per slide utilizing HALO image-analysis software. All FOVs underwent quality control (QC) by an independent team member to ensure placement of FOVs was consistent throughout slides.

Network Training. Three models of cycleGANs were trained for the image transformation from triplex to SPx Dabsyl, SPx TAMRA, and SPx Green, respectively. For each model, a total of 36 wholeslide images with annotated 180 FOVs of MPx and SPx images were used for training and testing. An FOV image was extracted to 36 patches of 256×256 images. The data were split to a train set, validation set, and a test set of 80%–10%–10%, respectively. The training/test split was performed subject-wise, in which the model was not exposed to any data from a specific subject during both training and testing phases. This approach aimed to enhance the generalization capability of the model by preventing it from becoming overly specialized to the characteristics of specific subjects and helped mitigate the risk of overfitting. As a result, there are a total of 5,184 image patches for the training set, 648 image patches for the validation set, 648 image patches for the test set. Of the three models, there are a total of 19,440 image patches. The hyperparameters for training were with a batch size of 4, a beta of 0.5, a learning rate of discriminators and generators of 0.0002, a learning rate decay iterations of 50, a learning rate policy with linear, a number of epochs of 200, a number of epochs decay of 100, and with Adam Optimizer.

4 Experiments and Results

4.1 Generated Synthesis Singleplex Images

As seen in Fig. 2B, 2C, and 2D, the output synthetic SPx images generated using our proposed framework from input triplex image in Fig. 2A. The reference images in Fig. 2E, 2F, and 2G are the corresponding adjacent SPx images referring as the intensity ground truth. The tissue morphology is not matched due to fact that they are adjacent slides, not the same slide. Thus, they have tissue morphology differences. As compared to the stain intensity levels, we can observe that the image quality and stain intensities of generated and real adjacent images look similar for all three SPx images. As shown in Fig. 2H, 2I and 2J, they are the corresponding synthetic SPx images generated using the conventional NMF methods, shown in poorer image quality and stain intensity levels.

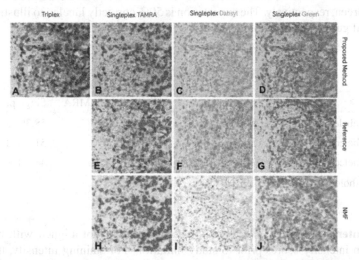

Fig. 2. (A) Input triplex image of CD3-Bcl2-CD8 with counterstain, (B) output synthetic SPx TAMRA or CD3 with counterstain, (C) output synthetic SPx Dabsyl or CD8 with counterstain, (D) output synthetic SPx Green or Bcl2 with counterstain, (E) real adjacent SPx TAMRA, (F) real adjacent SPx Dabsyl, (G) real adjacent SPx Green, (H) SPx TAMRA using NMF unmixing, (I) SPx Dabsyl using NMF unmixing, and (J) SPx Green using NMF unmixing. The image quality and stain intensities of generated and adjacent images look similar for all three SPx images, whereas the conventional NMF results show poorer image quality and stain intensity levels. The image resolution was 54×54 mm. (Color figure online)

4.2 Metric of Synthetic Image Evaluation

Evaluating the quality of synthetic images is an open and difficult problem. To evaluate the visual quality of our SPx images, we applied three experiments. First, we performed a perceptual study or "real vs. fake" based on Amazon Mechanical Turk (AMT) [10]. Three pathologists were expert observers in the experiments. Second, we evaluated whether our synthetic SPx images were realistic enough to be scored for intensity. The pathologist scored stain intensity without knowing that the image was synthetic or real. Finally, we evaluated synthetic SPx intensity by comparing the ground truth intensity of real adjacent SPx images in the optical density space.

Perceptual Studies. A total of 60 SPx images were presented to a pathologist with a series of trials that pitted a "real" image against a "syn" (synthetic) image generated using a triplex image. On each trial, each image appeared and Pathologist was given unlimited time to respond whether the image is "real" or "syn." Twenty images of each SPx i.e., TAMRA, Dabsyl, Green were given for feedback. As shown in Table 1, the analysis of the AMT results showed that the three pathologists correctly labeled for an average of 58.3% ± 6.7%, 61.7% ± 5.8%, and 58.3% ± 10.2%, for SPx Dabsyl, SPx TAMRA, and SPx Green, respectively. Moreover, the pathologists labeled syn on average of 50.0% ± 5.8%, 48.3% ± 3.5%, 51.7% ± 5.1%, for SPx Dabsy, SPx TAMRA, and SPx Green, respectively. The expectation is 50% correctly labeled to illustrate 50/50 syn vs. real guessing by pathologists.

Table 1. The analysis of the AMT perceptual study results

Results	Singleplex Dabsyl	Singleplex TAMRA	Singleplex Green
% Path* Labeled Correctly	58.3% ± 6.7%	61.7% ± 5.8%	58.3% ± 10.2%
% Path Labeled Syn	50.0% ± 5.8%	48.3% ± 3.5%	51.7% ± 5.1%
% Path Labeled Real	50.0% ± 5.8%	51.7% ± 3.5%	48.3% ± 5.1%

Path* = Pathologists.

Overall Intensity Scores. The three pathologists were not aligned with respect to chromogen intensity scores prior to study initiation. For staining intensity, the scores were ranked from 0–3 and any comments were captured. Readers were not provided with an appropriately stained DAB slide for comparison. Figure 3 shows the plots compared the overall intensity scores of SPx Dabsyl, SPx TAMRA, and SPx Green performed by three pathologists on both real and synthetic images.

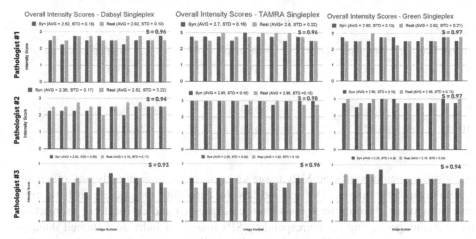

Fig. 3. The overall intensity scores of SPx Dabsyl, TAMRA, and Green performed by three pathologists on both real and synthetic images. The quantitative metric of Similarity $(S) = 1 - abs(n_1 - n_2) / (n_1 + n_2)$ ranking from 0.93–0.98 illustrates that the overall intensity scores are very similar for both real and synthetic images.

4.3 Comparison of Stain Intensities

We compared optical density (OD) between synthetic and adjacent SPx images. Each SPx image was unmixed using the NMF method. Then, the OD histograms were computed with the histogram correlation function. The OD histogram correlations of synthetic and adjacent SPx images were computed and compared, as shown in Table 2.

Table 2. The comparison of OD histogram correlations of synthetic and adjacent SPx images

Image Pair	Singleplex Dabsyl	Singleplex TAMRA	Singleplex Green
1	0.98	0.98	0.98
2	0.97	0.99	0.99
3	0.97	0.99	0.96
4	0.96	0.99	0.98
5	0.95	0.99	0.96
6	0.82	0.98	0.99

(continued)

5 Discussion and Conclusions

In overall, pathologists provided feedback that the synthetic SPx closely mirrored the adjacent, real SPx, and it was very hard to determine whether the image was synthetic or real. In most cases, they were not sure so it was their best impression. Our framework

Table 2. (*continued*)

Image Pair	Singleplex Dabsyl	Singleplex TAMRA	Singleplex Green
7	0.93	0.99	0.99
8	0.87	0.99	0.94
9	0.98	0.99	0.97
10	0.97	0.99	0.97

can virtually unmix stains on MPx tissue slides in order to accurately and efficiently generate synthetic images. Our method has the capability to generate realistic color distributions and decompose signals from co-expressed and co-localized biomarkers, for example, generating the corresponding SPx images of individual stained intensity for each biomarker from MPx images, similar to obtaining unmixed SPx images. The integration of our deep-learning image-based solutions with pathology can contribute exciting changes to health care, including: 1) eliminating the need for serial sections or re-staining, 2) providing tissue morphology matched images with realistic staining intensities, 3) resolving the limitation of conventional unmixing methods, and 4) improving the robustness and efficiency to provide to an applicable diagnosis.

The potential limitations posed by the small dataset size and acknowledging that the study's findings are based on a single scanner type. Future work could consider expanding the dataset size to enhance the reliability and credibility of the results. This would allow for more comprehensive and nuanced insights into participants' perceptions and evaluations. Our framework can generate synthetic images using unpaired images of triplex and real singleplex. This framework can be an alternative method and overcomes the limitations of the conventional unmixing method.

References

1. Morrison, L.E., Lefever, M.R., Behman, L.J., Leibold, T., Roberts, E.A., Horchner, U.B., et al.: Brightfield multiplex immunohistochemistry with multispectral imaging. Lab. Invest. **100**, 1124–1136 (2020)
2. Tan, W.C.C., Nerurkar, S.N., Cai, H.Y., Ng, H.H.M., Wu, D., Wee, Y.T.F., et al.: Overview of multiplex im-munohistochemistry/immunofluorescence techniques in the era of cancer immunotherapy. Cancer Commun. **40**, 135–153 (2020)
3. Joensuu, K., Leidenius, M., Kero, M., Andersson, L.C., Horwitz, K.B., Heikkilä, P.: ER, PR, HER2, Ki-67 and CK5 in early and late relapsing breast cancer-reduced CK5 expression in metastases. Breast Cancer (Auckl). **7**, 23–34 (2013)
4. Ruifrok, A.C., Johnston, D.A.: Quantification of histochemical staining by color deconvolution. J. Chem. Inf. Model **53**, 1689–1699 (2013)
5. Zhang, J., Zhang, X., Jiao, L.: Sparse Nonnegative Matrix Factorization for Hyperspectral Unmixing Based on Endmember Independence and Spatial Weighted Abundance. Remote Sens (Basel), vol. 13 (2021)
6. Bouteldja, N., Hölscher, D.L., Bülow, R.D., Roberts, I.S.D., Coppo, R., Boor, P.: Tackling stain variability using CycleGAN-based stain augmentation. J. Pathol. Inform. **13**, 100140 (2022)

7. Kapil, A., , et al.: DASGAN -- Joint Do-main Adaptation and Segmentation for the Analysis of Epithelial Regions in Histopathology PD-L1 Images. Comput. Vis. Pattern Recogn (2019)

8. Gadermayr, M., Gupta, L., Klinkhammer, B.M., Boor, P., Merhof, D.: Unsupervisedly training GANs for segmenting digital pathology with automatically generated annotations. In: ISBI (2019)

9. Gupta, L., Klinkhammer, B.M., Boor, P., Merhof, D., Gadermayr, M.: GAN-based image enrichment in digital pathology boosts segmentation accuracy. In: Medical Image Computing and Computer Assisted Intervention – MICCAI 2019, pp. 631–639. Springer International Publishing, Cham (2019). https://doi.org/10.1007/978-3-030-32239-7_70

10. Isola, P., Zhu, J.-Y., Zhou, T., Efros, A.A.: Image-to-Image Translation with Conditional Adversarial Networks (2016)

11. Zhao, Y., Ruihai, Wu., Dong, H.: Unpaired image-to-image translation using adversarial consistency loss. In: Vedaldi, A., Bischof, H., Brox, T., Frahm, J.-M. (eds.) Computer Vision – ECCV 2020: 16th European Conference, Glasgow, UK, August 23–28, 2020, Proceedings, Part IX, pp. 800–815. Springer International Publishing, Cham (2020). https://doi.org/10.1007/978-3-030-58545-7_46

12. Zhang, W., Hubbard, A., Jones, T., Racolta, A., Bhaumik, S., Cummins, N., et al.: Fully automated 5-plex fluorescent immunohistochemistry with tyramide signal amplification and same species anti-bodies. Lab. Invest. 97, 873–885 (2017)

Self-Supervised Super-Resolution for Anisotropic MR Images with and Without Slice Gap

Samuel W. Remedios[1,2(✉)], Shuo Han[3], Lianrui Zuo[4,5], Aaron Carass[4], Dzung L. Pham[6], Jerry L. Prince[4], and Blake E. Dewey[7]

[1] Department of Computer Science, Johns Hopkins University, Baltimore, MD 21218, USA
samuel.remedios@jhu.edu
[2] Department of Radiology and Imaging Sciences, National Institutes of Health, Bethesda, MD 20892, USA
[3] Department of Biomedical Engineering, Johns Hopkins School of Medicine, Baltimore, MD 21218, USA
[4] Department of Electrical and Computer Engineering, Johns Hopkins School of Medicine, Baltimore, MD 21218, USA
[5] Laboratory of Behavioral Neuroscience, National Institute on Aging, National Institutes of Health, Baltimore, MD 21224, USA
[6] Department of Radiology and Radiological Sciences, Uniformed Services University of the Health Sciences, Bethesda, MD 20892, USA
[7] Department of Neurology, Johns Hopkins School of Medicine, Baltimore, MD 21205, USA

Abstract. Magnetic resonance (MR) images are often acquired as multi-slice volumes to reduce scan time and motion artifacts while improving signal-to-noise ratio. These slices often are thicker than their in-plane resolution and sometimes are acquired with gaps between slices. Such thick-slice image volumes (possibly with gaps) can impact the accuracy of volumetric analysis and 3D methods. While many super-resolution (SR) methods have been proposed to address thick slices, few have directly addressed the slice gap scenario. Furthermore, data-driven methods are sensitive to domain shift due to the variability of resolution, contrast in acquisition, pathology, and differences in anatomy. In this work, we propose a self-supervised SR technique to address anisotropic MR images with and without slice gap. We compare against competing methods and validate in both signal recovery and downstream task performance on two open-source datasets and show improvements in all respects. Our code publicly available at https://gitlab.com/iacl/smore.

Keywords: super-resolution · MRI · self-supervised · deep learning

1 Introduction

Clinical acquisition with magnetic resonance (MR) imaging often uses 2D protocols where slices have a specified thickness and separation. When the slice thick-

J. M. Wolterink et al. (Eds.): SASHIMI 2023, LNCS 14288, pp. 118–128, 2023.
https://doi.org/10.1007/978-3-031-44689-4_12

ness and separation are greater than the in-plane resolution, the volume is said to be "anisotropic." When the separation between slices surpasses the thickness, then the volume is said to have "slice gap." Although anisotropic acquisitions are sufficient for trained radiologists to interpret and make diagnoses, automated algorithms often only perform reliably on isotropic resolutions. Thus, additional steps are needed to process the vast amount of clinical data accurately.

Super-resolution (SR) methods were proposed to address this problem by restoring anisotropic volumes to match their isotropic counterparts; that is, mapping low-resolution (LR) to high-resolution (HR). For example, [1] proposed to train a model using a paired HR-LR dataset and use that model to perform super-resolution. However, training a model using a paired HR-LR dataset requires having a testing dataset with a contrast and resolution consistent with the training data.

To confront these issues, self-supervised methods have seen increased interest. These are methods that use the input LR anisotropic image as a means of training an individualized model. In [11], a self-supervised two-stage method was trained to encourage cycle-consistency using a transformer-based model. In [21], an SR method was proposed to learn an implicit neural representation (INR), granting the ability to do arbitrary-scale SR. Similarly, [19] was also self-supervised and learned an INR, but required multiple anisotropic views of the same volume.

Another approach to self-supervision took advantage of the inherently higher in-plane high-resolution data to simulate paired HR-LR data. In [22] (SMORE), in-plane patches are extracted and degraded to form paired data, and two EDSR [10] networks are trained to remove aliasing and apply SR, respectively. In [13], a similar method is proposed, involving pre-training a set of networks and fine-tuning on the image at hand. In fact, SMORE [22] recommends using a pre-trained network as well and fine-tunes this model on the input LR volume, since purely self-supervised (i.e., no pre-training) performance is comparatively worse. However, despite great progress in SR for anisotropic volumes, the slice gap scenario has not been directly addressed.

Our work is inspired by SMORE but makes multiple key improvements. We utilize ESPRESO [3] to estimate the point spread function (PSF) from the input data, allowing us to model slice thickness independently of slice separation, directly addressing slice gap. We then use the WDSR architecture [20] (which is both more performant and lightweight than EDSR) that leverages pixel shuffle [17], and residual image prediction for more robust performance.

2   Methods

Slice thickness is often modeled as the full-width-at-half-max of the PSF and slice spacing is modeled as the distance between samples. A "slice gap" occurs when the slice spacing is greater than the slice thickness. We denote a slice thickness of Tmm and a slice gap of Gmm by $T\|G$ as in Remedios et. al [16]. The slice separation is $s = T + G$ and, since in practical scenarios slice thickness and slice gap are continuous values, s is generally not an integer.

Self-supervision for SR involves modeling both a forward and reverse processes for acquisition. That is, first we must learn how to create LR signals from HR before we learn to create HR signals from LR. Since our proposed method does not rely on external training data, the only available HR data are the in-plane slices. To increase the amount of available training data, we consider 2D *patches* rather than full slices for training.

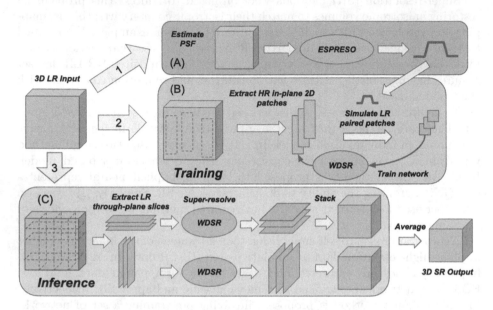

Fig. 1. An illustration of the proposed method. The input volume is anisotropic and is first passed into ESPRESO to get an estimate of the PSF (A). Then, during training 2D patches are extracted from the HR in-plane slices, blurred with the estimated PSF, and downsampled to match the slice spacing. This sets up paired training data to train the WDSR network (B). Finally, at inference time (C), the LR through-plane slices are extracted from the input volume and are super-resolved with the trained WDSR before being stacked and averaged, resulting in an isotropic output volume.

2.1   The Forward Process: HR → LR

Both slice thickness and slice separation must be modeled in the forward process. Contemporary SR techniques for anisotropic MR images model the forward process as either direct B-spline downsampling [11,13,21] or a convolution with a blur kernel (typically Gaussian) to model the PSF before subsampling [7,22,23]. The latter is more apt for modeling 2D MR acquisition since it considers the slice thickness and separation independently. Rather than assuming a particular form of the PSF, we use ESPRESO [3,4] to estimate the slice selection profile. Briefly, this self-supervised method optimizes a blur kernel adversarially such that, after application, degraded in-plane patches match the distribution of observed through-plane patches. This is illustrated in Fig. 1 (A). After convolution with the estimated PSF, we model slice separation with cubic B-spline interpolation.

2.2   The Reverse Process: LR → HR

With a model of the forward process, traditional supervised machine learning techniques can be applied to address the reverse process. At train time, Fig. 1 (B), 2D patches are extracted from in-plane and paired {LR, HR} data are now available to train a network. At inference time, Fig. 1 (C), we follow a similar process as training time, but apply the model to all through-plane slices extracted from both cardinal directions before stacking and averaging to produce the final output. We selected WDSR [20] (specifically WDSR-B, which we will refer to as WDSR for the remainder of this work) as our architecture due to its empirical improvement over EDSR and RCAN as an SR backbone. In summary, this network is lightweight, features the "wide activation", uses weight normalization rather than batch normalization, estimates the residual between the input image (after spline interpolation and pixel shuffle to the correct digital grid) and the target HR image, and uses pixel shuffle [17] rather than conventional upsample-convolve or transposed convolution layers. However, in practice the slice separation s may not be an integer, which is a necessary condition for pixel shuffle. To address this, we first interpolate with a cubic B-spline to the nearest integer before running data through the network. Precisely, given a slice separation s, the first cubic interpolation is at a factor $\tilde{s} = s/\lfloor s \rfloor$, and the pixel shuffle upscaling is at the factor $\lfloor s \rfloor$, where $\lfloor \cdot \rfloor$ is the floor operation.

Training. The training data creation details are as follows. First, the LR input volume is linearly normalized to $[0, 1]$ by the minimum and maximum intensity values. The slice separation, s, is assumed to be known, typically defined by the image header. To account for boundary effects when applying the PSF, the LR image is reflect-padded along the in-plane cardinal axes by an extension $e = 2\lceil L/2 \rceil$, where L is the array length of the estimated PSF and $\lceil \cdot \rceil$ is the ceiling operation. To increase the amount of available training data, the volume undergoes several basic augmentations in-plane: horizontal flips, vertical flips, and 90 degree rotation. Second, 2D HR in-plane patches are extracted of size $(48 + e) \times (48 + e)s$. Patches may be extracted from any of the augmented LR volumes. The probability of pulling a particular patch is weighted by its image gradient magnitude, so patches with many edge features are more likely to be sampled. Third, once a patch is extracted, it is blurred via convolution with the PSF estimated from ESPRESO. Fourth, the extended HR patch size is cropped down to $48 \times 48s$ to remove boundary effects. Finally, the patches are downsampled with cubic B-spline interpolation by a factor of s. This process yields paired {LR, HR} patches of grid sizes 48×48 and $48 \times 48s$ respectively.

Equipped with paired training data, we train the aforementioned WDSR architecture with the L1 loss, the OneCycle learning rate scheduler [18], and automatic mixed precision with a batch size of 32. Training continued until the model "saw" $832,000$ patches, an empirically found stopping point based on [2].

Inference. We apply the trained model to all 2D through-plane slices extracted from the cardinal axes. For example, if the LR volume was axially acquired, then we super-resolve all sagittal and coronal slices. Slices super-resolved in this way are re-stacked into their respective estimated volumes and the final output is the arithmetic mean of the two. Since the model was trained on intensities $[0, 1]$, we first linearly normalize the LR volume exactly as in training. After application of the model, we invert this normalization to return to the original intensity range.

There is one extra complication during inference compared to training. Recall that pixel shuffle maps integer to integer. Let N be the number of in-plane slices in the LR volume. Ideally, we would like to have $\lfloor Ns \rceil$ slices in our SR volume, where $\lfloor \cdot \rceil$ is the round operation. The network, however, first interpolates to the nearest integer, then applies pixel shuffle. Recalling our two-stage interpolation to obtain the correct number of slices, $\tilde{s} = s/\lfloor s \rfloor$ is a first-step B-spline interpolation and $\lfloor s \rfloor$ is pixel shuffle upsampling. However, since $\tilde{s}$ may not be integer, practically this value is rounded; thus, the first interpolation is by $\lfloor N\tilde{s} \rceil$. It is not guaranteed that $\lfloor N\tilde{s} \rceil \lfloor s \rfloor$ equals $\lfloor Ns \rceil$. Therefore, we look to pad the image by p such that all operations yield integer values and we have the ideal number of SR slices. Concisely:

$$\underbrace{\overbrace{\lfloor (N+p)\tilde{s} \rceil}^{} \times \overbrace{\lfloor s \rfloor}^{\text{Pixel shuffle scaling}} - \underbrace{\lfloor ps \rceil}_{}}_{\substack{\text{Pre-network interpolation} \\ \text{Remove scaled padding}}} = \overbrace{\lfloor Ns \rceil}^{\text{Ideal number of SR slices}} . \qquad (1)$$

We find this numerically, searching through $p = 0, 1, \ldots, 1000$ and keep p such that the distance between the LHS and RHS of Eq. 1 is minimal. In our experiments, we were always able to find a p which yields exactly the correct number of slices.

3 Experiments

To evaluate our method, we considered two disparate open-source datasets with respective downstream tasks and eight resolutions. The eight resolutions were $3\|0, 3\|1, 4\|0, 4\|1, 4\|1.2, 5\|0, 5\|1, 5\|1.5$, the most common clinical resolutions for 2D MRI [14]. Both experiments investigated all eight of these resolutions by simulation. Simulation of $T\|G$ LR data was conducted via convolution of the HR data in the through-plane direction with a slice-selection profile of thickness Tmm via Shinnar-Le Roux pulse design [12] and a slice separation of $T + G$mm obtained with cubic B-spline subsampling.

The first dataset-task pair was anatomical brain region segmentation of $N = 50$ randomly selected T_1-w MRI from the OASIS-3 dataset [8]. Each subject at each resolution was upsampled with cubic B-spline interpolation, super-resolved with SMORE [22], SynthSR [6], and our proposed method. Then, the result

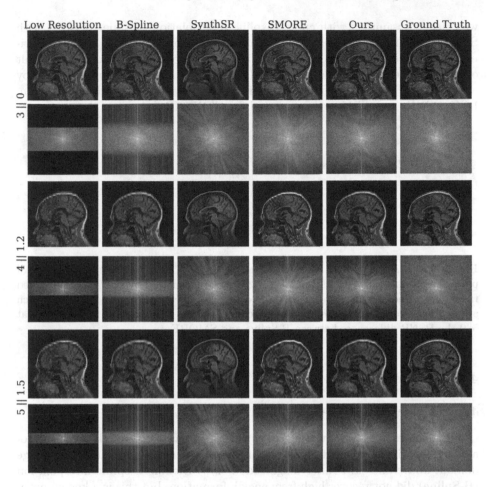

Fig. 2. A mid-sagittal through-plane slice from a representative subject after applying each method at three selected resolutions. Each pair of rows depicts the MR slice above and its Fourier magnitude below. From left-to-right: the low resolution image, cubic B-spline interpolation, SynthSR, SMORE, our proposed approach, and the true high resolution image.

of each method (alongside the HR ground truth) was automatically segmented by SLANT [5] and the resultant labels were reduced for simplicity following Remedios et. al [15]: ventricles, cerebellar GM, cerebellar WM, cerebral GM, cerebral WM, caudate, putamen, thalamus, and brainstem. Evaluation of each method was conducted in terms of Dice similarity coefficient (DSC) between the HR segmentations (i.e., "silver-standard") and the SR segmentations as well as in terms of signal recovery using peak signal-to-noise-ratio (PSNR) and structural similarity (SSIM), computed with the `skimage.metrics` module.

The second dataset-task pair was multiple sclerosis (MS) brain lesion segmentation of $N = 30$ FLAIR MRI from the 3D-MR-MS dataset [9]. Each subject was either upsampled with cubic B-spline interpolation or super-resolved with SMORE or our proposed method. SynthSR was not applicable in this experiment since it does not produce FLAIR images nor retain MS lesions. The result of each SR method and the HR ground truth were automatically segmented by a pre-trained U-net to produce a binary mask of white matter lesions. Again, DSC, PSNR, and SSIM were computed for all SR-HR pairs.

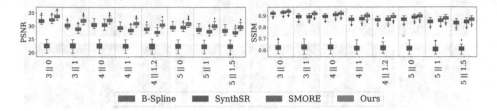

Fig. 3. PSNR and SSIM for the OASIS-3 dataset ($N = 50$) across each resolution. All pairs per resolution are significant with $p \ll 0.01$ as calculated by the Wilcoxon signed rank task without correction for multiple comparisons except for the following which are not significant: at 4∥0 the PSNR differences between B-Spline and SMORE and at 5∥0 the PSNR differences between B-Spline and SMORE.

4   Results

4.1   Dataset 1: OASIS-3

Qualitative results are shown in Fig. 2, which compared a through-plane slice of a representative subject at three resolutions. Each resolution shows the image domain above and its Fourier magnitude below. Bicubic B-spline interpolation (B-Spline) did not recover high frequency information, but this is a known property of interpolation methods. SynthSR mapped the LR image to its training range, but in the process worsens some high-frequency signal along the in-plane axes as well. Additionally, note that while OASIS-3 images are MPRAGE (the training range of SynthSR), the contrast was not identical to the ground truth image. Results outside the brain were also not comparable, since SynthSR is intended for brain regions primarily. Both SMORE and our proposed approach retained in-plane frequency information and recovered some through-plane information.

Signal recovery quantitative results are shown in Fig. 3. Our proposed method outperformed the comparison methods at all resolutions in both metrics. Downstream task quantitative results are shown in Fig. 4 for the nine simplified SLANT regions. All pairs per resolution were significant for all regions according to the Wilcoxon signed rank text with $p \ll 0.01$ except for the following: in the brainstem at 3∥0, 4∥0, 5∥0 between SMORE and Ours, in the caudate at 3∥1 between B-Spline and SMORE, in the caudate at 4∥1.2 between SMORE and

Ours, in the putamen at 3‖0 between SMORE and Ours, in the putamen at 4‖1.2 between B-Spline and Ours, and in the cerebellar white matter at 3‖1, 4‖0, 5‖1 between SMORE and Ours.

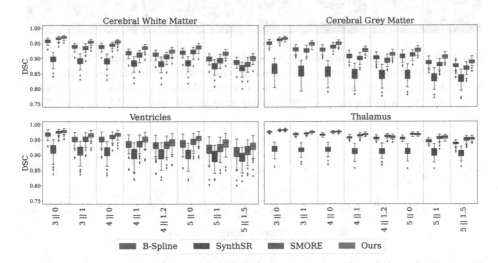

Fig. 4. DSC for four representative brain regions across each resolution for the OASIS-3 dataset ($N = 50$). In this figure, all pairs per resolution are significant for all regions according to the Wilcoxon signed rank text with $p \ll 0.01$ except for cerebellar white matter at 3‖1, 4‖0, 5‖1 between SMORE and Ours. For significance testing of the other five regions not shown in this figure, see the main text.

4.2   Dataset 2: 3D-MR-MS

A representative comparison between SR and lesion segmentations across methods is shown in Fig. 5, with the binary mask overlaid in orange. Qualitatively there were two important features to compare across the resultant super-resolved MR images. First, although SMORE appeared to be sharper, it exhibited a kind of "over-sharpening," as shown in the regions indicated by the yellow arrows. Second, our proposed method better recovered a surface between the brain and skull in the mid-superior area of the head. Now considering the segmentations qualitatively, although no method compared to the segmentation of the ground truth, SMORE and B-Spline both had more false negatives than our approach. Quantitative results are shown in Fig. 6. The Wilcoxon signed rank test indicated that differences between all pairs per resolution were significant ($p \ll 0.01$), but without corrections for multiple comparisons.

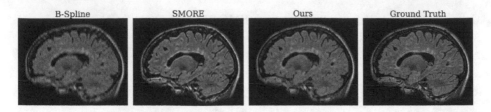

Fig. 5. A representative through-plane sagittal slice and overlaid automated segmentation at 3∥1. Yellow arrows indicate areas where SMORE "oversharpens" the signal by introducing a hyperintensity inferior to an edge. Magenta arrows indicate a failure of SMORE to recover a surface, whereas our approach is more faithful. (Color figure online)

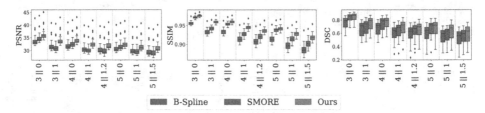

Fig. 6. PSNR, SSIM, and DSC for the 3D-MR-MS dataset ($N = 30$) at each resolution. All pairs per resolution are significant ($p \ll 0.01$) according to the Wilcoxon signed rank test.

5   Conclusions

In this work, we have proposed an improved method for addressing thick slices with and without slice gap in anisotropic MR images via self-supervised super-resolution. Our proposed method was the best performing in terms of signal recovery across all tasks and resolutions, and was the best performing in two disparate downstream segmentation tasks in all but two scenarios: thalamus segmentation at resolutions 4∥1.2 and 5∥0, where it was second best.

The qualitative Fourier magnitude shown in Fig. 2 shows that all compared SR methods have a long way to go in terms of recovery of the high frequency signal. SynthSR is consistent across all resolutions, but worsens in-plane resolution as well. Both SMORE and our approach recover more signal than present in the original LR anisotropic volume, but neither are close to recovering the entire spectrum. Future work will investigate whether this shortcoming is due to the training scheme (maximum a priori), data quality (self-supervision vs supervised with a large dataset), model paradigm (convolutional neural net vs GAN or DDPM), or something else.

Our contributions included a streamlined and more robust self-supervised training and inference scheme, an optimized architecture, and thorough evaluation on two different datasets with two different downstream tasks, revealing improved quantitative performance across several clinical resolutions (some with slice gaps as well) for each dataset.

Acknowledgements. This material is supported by the National Science Foundation Graduate Research Fellowship under Grant No. DGE-1746891 (Remedios). Development is partially supported by NIH ORIP grant R21 OD030163 (Pham). This work also received support from National Multiple Sclerosis Society RG-1907-34570 (Pham), FG-2008-36966 (Dewey), CDMRP W81XWH2010912 (Prince), and the Department of Defense in the Center for Neuroscience and Regenerative Medicine. The opinions and assertions expressed herein are those of the authors and do not reflect the official policy or position of the Uniformed Services University of the Health Sciences or the Department of Defense.

References

1. Du, J., et al.: Super-resolution reconstruction of single anisotropic 3D MR images using residual convolutional neural network. Neurocomputing **392**, 209–220 (2020)
2. Han, S.: Cerebellum parcellation from magnetic resonance imaging using deep learning. PhD thesis, Johns Hopkins University, Baltimore, MD (2022)
3. Han, S., Remedios, S., Carass, A., Schär, M., Prince, J.L.: MR slice profile estimation by learning to match internal patch distributions. In: Feragen, A., Sommer, S., Schnabel, J., Nielsen, M. (eds.) IPMI 2021. LNCS, vol. 12729, pp. 108–119. Springer, Cham (2021). https://doi.org/10.1007/978-3-030-78191-0_9
4. Han, S., Remedios, S.W., Schär, M., Carass, A., Prince, J.L.: ESPRESO: an algorithm to estimate the slice profile of a single magnetic resonance image. Magn. Reson. Imaging **98**, 155–163 (2023)
5. Huo, Y., Xu, Z., Xiong, Y., Aboud, K., Parvathaneni, P., Bao, S., Bermudez, C., Resnick, S.M., Cutting, L.E., Landman, B.A.: 3D whole brain segmentation using spatially localized atlas network tiles. Neuroimage **194**, 105–119 (2019)
6. Iglesias, J.E., et al.: SynthSR: a public AI tool to turn heterogeneous clinical brain scans into high-resolution T1-weighted images for 3D morphometry. Sci. Adv. **9**(5), eadd3607 (2023)
7. Krishnan, A.P., Upendra, R.R., Pramanik, A., Song, Z., Carano, R.A., Initiative, A.D.N.: Multimodal super resolution with dual domain loss and gradient guidance. In: Simulation and Synthesis in Medical Imaging: 7th International Workshop, SASHIMI 2022, Held in Conjunction with MICCAI 2022, Singapore, September 18, 2022, Proceedings, pp. 91–100. Springer (2022). https://doi.org/10.1007/978-3-031-16980-9_9
8. LaMontagne, P.J., et al.: OASIS-3: longitudinal neuroimaging, clinical, and cognitive dataset for normal aging and alzheimer disease. medRxiv (2019)
9. Lesjak, Ž., et al.: A novel public MR image dataset of multiple sclerosis patients with lesion segmentations based on multi-rater consensus. Neuroinformatics **16**, 51–63 (2018)
10. Lim, B., Son, S., Kim, H., Nah, S., Mu Lee, K.: Enhanced deep residual networks for single image super-resolution. In: Proceedings of the IEEE Conference on Computer Vision and Pattern Recognition Workshops, pp. 136–144 (2017)
11. Lu, Z., et al.: Two-stage self-supervised cycle-consistency transformer network for reducing slice gap in MR images. IEEE J. Biomed. Health Inform. **27**(7), 3337–3348 (2023)

12. Martin, J., Ong, F., Ma, J., Tamir, J.I., Lustig, M., Grissom, W.A.: SigPy.RF: comprehensive open-source RF pulse design tools for reproducible research. In: Proceedings of the International Society for Magnetic Resonance in Medicine. ISMRM Annual Meeting, vol. 1045 (2020)

13. Peng, C., Zhou, S.K., Chellappa, R.: DA-VSR: domain adaptable volumetric super-resolution for medical images. In: de Bruijne, M., et al. (eds.) MICCAI 2021. LNCS, vol. 12906, pp. 75–85. Springer, Cham (2021). https://doi.org/10.1007/978-3-030-87231-1_8

14. Remedios, S.W., et al.: Cautions in anisotropy: thick slices and slice gaps in 2D magnetic resonance acquisition tarnish volumetrics. Int. J. Multiple Sclerosis Care **25**, 55 (2023)

15. Remedios, S.W., Han, S., Dewey, B.E., Pham, D.L., Prince, J.L., Carass, A.: Joint image and label self-super-resolution. In: Svoboda, D., Burgos, N., Wolterink, J.M., Zhao, C. (eds.) SASHIMI 2021. LNCS, vol. 12965, pp. 14–23. Springer, Cham (2021). https://doi.org/10.1007/978-3-030-87592-3_2

16. Remedios, S.W., et al.: Deep filter bank regression for super-resolution of anisotropic MR brain images. In: Medical Image Computing and Computer Assisted Intervention-MICCAI 2022: 25th International Conference, Singapore, September 18–22, 2022, Proceedings, Part VI, pp. 613–622. Springer, Cham (2022). https://doi.org/10.1007/978-3-031-16446-0_58

17. Shi, W., et al.: Real-time single image and video super-resolution using an efficient sub-pixel convolutional neural network. In: Proceedings of the IEEE Conference on Computer Vision and Pattern Recognition, pp. 1874–1883 (2016)

18. Smith, L.N., Topin, N.: Super-convergence: very fast training of neural networks using large learning rates. In: Artificial Intelligence and Machine Learning for Multi-domain Operations Applications, vol. 11006, pp. 369–386. SPIE (2019)

19. Wu, Q., et al.: IREM: high-resolution magnetic resonance image reconstruction via implicit neural representation. In: de Bruijne, M., et al. (eds.) MICCAI 2021. LNCS, vol. 12906, pp. 65–74. Springer, Cham (2021). https://doi.org/10.1007/978-3-030-87231-1_7

20. Yu, J., Fan, Y., Yang, J., Xu, N., Wang, X., Huang, T.S.: Wide activation for efficient and accurate image super-resolution. arXiv preprint arXiv:1808.08718 (2018)

21. Zhang, H., et al.: Self-supervised arbitrary scale super-resolution framework for anisotropic MRI. arXiv preprint arXiv:2305.01360 (2023)

22. Zhao, C., Dewey, B.E., Pham, D.L., Calabresi, P.A., Reich, D.S., Prince, J.L.: SMORE: a self-supervised anti-aliasing and super-resolution algorithm for MRI using deep learning. IEEE Trans. Med. Imaging **40**(3), 805–817 (2020)

23. Zhao, C., et al.: Applications of a deep learning method for anti-aliasing and super-resolution in MRI. Magn. Reson. Imaging **64**, 132–141 (2019)

DIFF·3: A Latent Diffusion Model for the Generation of Synthetic 3D Echocardiographic Images and Corresponding Labels

Edward Ferdian[1,2]([⊠]), Debbie Zhao[1]([⊠]), Gonzalo D. Maso Talou[1],
Gina M. Quill[1], Malcolm E. Legget[3], Robert N. Doughty[3,4],
Martyn P. Nash[1,5], and Alistair A. Young[6]

[1] Auckland Bioengineering Institute, University of Auckland, Auckland, New Zealand
debbie.zhao@auckland.ac.nz
[2] Faculty of Informatics, Telkom University, Bandung, Indonesia
[3] Department of Medicine, University of Auckland, Auckland, New Zealand
[4] Green Lane Cardiovascular Service, Auckland City Hospital,
Auckland, New Zealand
[5] Department of Engineering Science and Biomedical Engineering, University of
Auckland, Auckland, New Zealand
[6] School of Biomedical Engineering and Imaging Sciences, King's College London,
London, UK

Abstract. Large amounts of labelled data are typically needed to develop robust deep learning methods for medical image analysis. However, issues related to the high costs of acquisition, time-consuming analysis, and patient privacy, have limited the number of publicly available datasets. Recently, latent diffusion models have been employed to generate synthetic data in several fields. Compared to other imaging modalities, the manipulation of 3D echocardiograms is particularly challenging due to the higher dimensionality and complex noise characteristics, and lack of objective ground truth. We present DIFF·3, a latent diffusion model for synthesizing realistic 3D echocardiograms with high-quality labels from matching cardiovascular magnetic resonance imaging (CMR) scans. Using *in vivo* 3D echocardiograms from 134 participants and corresponding registered labels derived from CMR, source images and labels are initially compressed by a variational autoencoder, followed by diffusion in the latent space. Synthetic datasets were subsequently generated by randomly sampling from the latent distribution, and evaluated in terms of fidelity and diversity. DIFF·3 may provide an effective and more efficient means of generating labelled 3D echocardiograms to supplement real patient data.

Keywords: Latent diffusion · 3D echocardiography · Deep learning · Generative AI · Synthetic data

E. Ferdian and D. Zhao—Joint first authorship.
M. P. Nash and A. A. Young—Joint senior authorship.

J. M. Wolterink et al. (Eds.): SASHIMI 2023, LNCS 14288, pp. 129–140, 2023.
https://doi.org/10.1007/978-3-031-44689-4_13

1   Introduction

The application of deep learning for automated medical image analysis and interpretation typically requires access to large labelled datasets to ensure good performance and generalizability. Nevertheless, data paucity remains a challenge in this domain due to the high costs associated with acquisition and time-consuming analysis, as well as concerns related to data privacy. Furthermore, the variability associated with manual annotations adversely impact the reliability of ground truth labels. As a result, the number of publicly available datasets with high-quality labels that can be used for the development of data-driven methods for automated analysis are limited.

Echocardiography is the most widely used modality for cardiac assessment, and deep learning models for automated analysis are being actively developed. Previous strategies to address the lack of training data have included the use of generative adversarial networks [7, 23], transfer learning [6, 17], as well as physical simulators combining electromechanical models [29] and ultrasound point scatters [2] to produce *in silico* echocardiograms. More recently, diffusion models inspired by non-equilibrium thermodynamics, have been proposed as a state-of-the-art method for the generation of realistic synthetic data. Diffusion models function by means of learning noise reversal, a process that enables coherent images to be recovered from randomly sampled noise. Such models have been employed in a variety of medical applications, including chest radiography [4], brain imaging [18], and histopathology [16].

In comparison to 2D images, the manipulation and handling of 3D data is more challenging due to the higher data dimensionality and computational memory requirements. Consequently, very few libraries and pre-trained weights have been made available for tasks associated with diffusion using 3D inputs [13]. Nevertheless, the acquisition and analysis of 3D data represents an important step forward for the derivation of accurate geometric representations of anatomy (such as for chamber volume quantification in echocardiography) without the need for the geometric assumptions present in 2D imaging.

Here, we present DIFF·3, a latent diffusion model (LDM) for the synthesis of realistic 3D echocardiograms with labels informed by cardiac magnetic resonance (CMR) imaging to provide a more efficient means of generating realistic and high-quality datasets. Contributions include: 1) a method for generating paired 3D images and labels; and 2) the use of paired high-quality ground truth segmentations from a more accurate modality (CMR).

2   Methods

2.1   Reference Dataset

To provide training data for DIFF·3, we leverage MITEA, a publicly available 3D echocardiography (3DE) dataset with subject-specific labels (of the left ventricular myocardium and cavity) derived from higher-resolution CMR [28]. This dataset consists of 536 annotated grey-scale 3DE images (of approximately

$167 \times 168 \times 132$ in size, with each dimension ranging between 101–243 voxels), acquired from 134 participants (4 images per subject). The same training and testing split was used as in the original publication, consisting of 428 and 108 paired images and labels (split by participant), respectively. For additional dataset characteristics, the reader is referred to the original publication [28].

Pre-processing. An input size of $160 \times 160 \times 128 \times 2$ was chosen as an approximate mean image size, with corresponding images and labels stacked in the channel dimension. Images with dimensions smaller than the target size were padded, while images larger than the input size were first down-sampled (using a cubic polynomial and nearest-neighbour interpolation scheme for images and labels, respectively), and subsequently padded to retain the aspect ratio. Voxel intensities were min-max normalized on a per-image basis.

2.2 Latent Diffusion Model

DIFF·3 consists of two separate networks. The first stage consists of a Variational Auto Encoder (VAE) which compresses the higher-dimensional 3DE data into a lower-dimensional latent space (z) following a prior Gaussian distribution. The second stage consists of a diffusion model, which learns a reverse diffusion process using deep neural networks. The forward diffusion process is a parameterized Markov chain where Gaussian noise is added in successive steps based on a variance schedule, until the original (target) data is corrupted. The reverse diffusion process minimizes the negative log-likelihood with respect to the target distribution. Consequently, the execution of diffusion models is a time-consuming and computationally expensive process, which requires sequential operations over a large number of time steps. To exploit the reduction in dimensionality while still providing efficient image generation capability, we used a Denoising Diffusion Probabilistic Model (DDPM) [9] in the second stage. Training and inference were performed on an NVIDIA A100 GPU with 80 GB of memory.

Variational Auto Encoder. An existing VAE model, which acts as a perceptual compression stage capable of learning semantic variations [19], was extended to handle 3D inputs (i.e., using 3D convolutions and attention layers) and trained to optimize reconstruction loss (comprising pixel-wise loss (L1) on the image channel, sparse cross-entropy loss on the label channel, and perceptual loss across both image and labels).

As pixel-space loss is known to produce blurry images due to high-frequency information being filtered out in the encoding process, perceptual loss was added by calculating features from five different stages of the VGG loss network. Due to the lack of available pre-trained 3D loss networks (e.g., VGG, AlexNet), we utilized 2D loss network (LPIPS) based on VGGNet [27], and deconstructed each 3D image into a grid of 2D axial, coronal, and sagittal slices (see Fig. 1). Although a 3D loss network (MedicalNet [3]) was available, this produced inferior results (i.e., blurrier images) compared with the 2D strategy upon visual inspection due to the model not being designed for perception tasks.

To ensure that the posterior distribution follows the prior Gaussian distribution, we regularize the latent space using the Kullback-Leibler (KL) term to be standard normal distributed. This resulted in latent dataset representations of size $20 \times 20 \times 16 \times 4$. The network was trained for 200 epochs with the following hyperparameters: batch size of 1, learning rate of $1e^{-4}$, and KL weight of $1e^{-6}$, to produce high-quality images. After 100 epochs, the KL weight was increased to 1 to further constrain the latent space distribution. Training time was approximately 5 min per epoch (or 15 h in total), and the best model was chosen based on the lowest validation reconstruction loss.

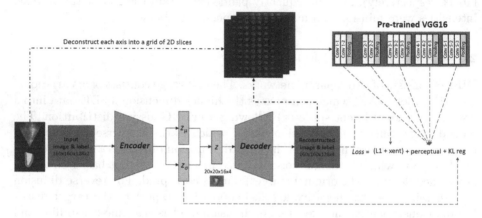

Fig. 1. A global overview of the first-stage Variational Auto Encoder network. The perceptual loss is computed using VGG-16 by deconstructing each 3D image into a grid of 2D slices for each of the 3 axes. (Note that only 1 axis is shown here.

Denoising Diffusion Probablistic Model. The latent representations of the reference dataset were used as training data for the second-stage network. The diffusion model was based on an existing *PyTorch* implementation [15], which was again adapted for 3D input data. The network architecture consists of a U-Net model with self-attention. A Gaussian diffusion scheduler was set to 1000 time steps based on a sigmoid function [12], and the network was trained for 50000 iterations using a pixel-loss objective function (L1) and a learning rate of $8e^{-5}$. All other hyperparameters were set to their default values, and the best model was chosen based on the lowest training loss. Owing to the small size of the latent input data ($20 \times 20 \times 16 \times 4$), it was possible to use a batch size of 64, with a training time of 0.9 s per iteration (resulting in a total training time of approximately 12 h).

2.3 Inference and Synthetic Data Generation

Sampling was performed in the latent space and generated using Denoising Diffusion Implicit Models (DDIM) [20] with 100 steps, which is a more efficient class of non-Markovian diffusion processes that can produce high-quality samples in fewer steps. Subsequently, these latent representations were passed on to the decoder of the first-stage network to reconstruct synthetic 3DE images. We generated 5000 synthetic images and labels for qualitative and quantitative evaluation. Inference time for the LDM and the subsequent VAE decoding step took approximately 0.31 s and 0.35 s per sample and image, respectively.

2.4 Validation and Performance

Model performance was evaluated based on the generated sample fidelity and diversity, using several metrics. We used the Fréchet Inception Distance (FID) [8] (calculated using an approach similar to [10,21]) to measure how realistic the synthetic images were, where a small FID indicated that the distribution of the synthetic images was similar to the distribution of the real images. To match the amount of data in the MITEA training set, 428 generated synthetic images were chosen randomly for evaluation. Improved precision (IP) and improved recall (IR) [14] of the generated synthetic data with respect to the training data were also evaluated, computed using the same 2048-dimensional feature vectors extracted using Inception V3 [26]. For comparison, FID, IP, and IR were also calculated for the test set against the training set belonging to MITEA.

To assess diversity, we used the multiscale structural similarity metric (MS-SSIM) by averaging the results on 428 images (214 pairs) of the same dataset, for both the synthetic and real training dataset, where higher MS-SSIM scores suggest that the images within the datasets are more similar [13]. Additionally, to visualize the distributions of the synthetic and training datasets, we utilized Locally Linear Embedding (LLE), a manifold learning framework to project the high-dimensional data into a lower-dimensional space.

Comparison to Generative Adversarial Network. To obtain baseline evaluation metrics for synthetic data generated by DIFF·3, we trained a previously published state-of-the-art 3D generative adversarial network (HA-GAN) [21] using two different supported resolutions (128^3 and 256^3). All other configurations were left unchanged.

Utility of Synthetic Data for Segmentation. Finally, to assess the utility of DIFF·3 for downstream tasks such as segmentation, the addition of synthetic data was used in the retraining of a deep learning network (nnU-Net [11]) for left ventricle segmentation. The segmentation network was trained using five-fold cross-validation with the same parameters and training/validation/testing splits as in the original MITEA publication [28].

3   Results

3.1   Qualitative Assessment

Figure 2 shows examples of real and synthetic paired 3DE images and labels from the MITEA training set and DIFF·3, respectively. From visual inspection, DIFF·3 was able to produce high-quality images and labels with realistic textures and speckle characteristics. A variety of ultrasound sector widths, left ventricular shapes, and realistic image artefacts were observed on the generated samples. In comparison, synthetic images generated by HA-GAN appeared to lack variation.

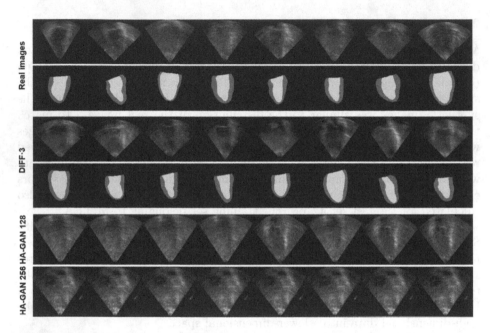

Fig. 2. Real and synthetic samples of 3D echocardiograms and their corresponding labels. Note that HA-GAN does not produce corresponding labels as it was trained unconditionally.

3.2   Quantitative Assessment

The capability of the VAE component was evaluated using the MITEA test set (n = 108) by comparing the reconstructed data to the original images and labels. The resultant Structural Similarity Index (as a measure of image quality degradation by compression) was was 0.84 ± 0.03, and the Dice coefficients for the left ventricular myocardium and cavity labels were 0.97 ± 0.01 and 0.99 ± 0.01, respectively.

The FID, IP, and IR scores for the synthetic and MITEA test data against the training data are shown in Table 1. The FID values were comparable between the synthetic and real test data, indicating a similar distance to the training data distribution. Furthermore, IP was high, with a moderate IR compared to that obtained by the real MITEA test data.

Table 1. Quantitative evaluation using Fréchet Inception Distance (FID), Improved Precision (IP), and Improved Recall (IR) for real MITEA test data, synthetic data generated using DIFF·3 and HA-GAN against the reference MITEA training dataset (n = 428).

Data	FID↓	IP↑	IR↑
Real (n = 108)	14.0	0.731	0.797
DIFF·3 (n = 428)	13.7	0.888	0.694
HA-GAN 128 (n = 428)	46.7	0.486	0.000
HA-GAN 256 (n = 428)	101.2	0.000	0.000

With respect to diversity, DIFF·3 achieved a lower MS-SSIM score of 0.710 compared to that of the training dataset (0.781), indicating greater diversity. In comparison, HA-GAN 128 and 256 produced MS-SSIM scores of 0.998 and 0.999, respectively, indicating low diversity (as MS-SSIM is inversely proportional to diversity). A visualization of the dataset distributions following LLE are shown in Fig. 3.

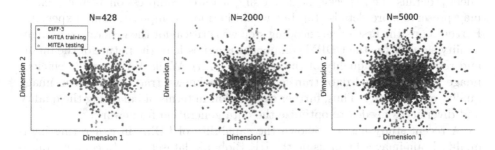

Fig. 3. Locally Linear Embedding of the real and generated synthetic images with n = 428, 2000, and 5000, respectively.

Based on the data distribution plots, 2000 synthetic samples were added to the original MITEA training data (such that each of the five folds had an addition of 400 synthetic image and label pairs). The number of synthetic samples was empirically chosen to cover the distribution seen to be spanned by the MITEA data. The resulting segmentation network produced Dice coefficients of 0.762

and 0.866 for the myocardium and cavity, respectively, which were marginally lower than the corresponding Dice coefficients of 0.766 and 0.871 when trained with real data only.

4   Discussion

With the advances in generative models, the synthesis of realistic synthetic data may help to address the data scarcity problem in the domain of medical imaging. Standard augmentation strategies (e.g., rotation, scaling, and mirroring), can help to add variations to the dataset. However, the resultant images lack diversity in terms of task-specific high-level semantic attributes, which are important for model generalizability. Meanwhile, the use of diffusion models to serve as an advanced augmentation strategy by synthesizing new data from the original data distribution has shown to improve accuracy in both medical and non-medical domains [1,24]. While synthetic images alone can serve several purposes, the simultaneous generation of labels can also provide readily available segmentations of the structures of interest without the requirement for manual labelling efforts or the associated variability. In our study, we leveraged the channel dimension as a novel approach for simultaneously generating corresponding ground truth labels.

Working with 3D images is challenging due to the additional computational requirements. The use of an LDM provided a way to lower the demand by first encoding the images into latent representations. We opted for a compression factor of 8 on each of the dimension (i.e., images of resolution $160 \times 160 \times 128$ to latent dimension of $20 \times 20 \times 16$), to account for the high dimensionality of the data. Consequently, there is a trade-off in the potential loss of high frequency details (i.e., speckle noise). Using a lower compression factor (i.e., 4) may preserve more details [13], but would be more computationally expensive. Furthermore, the first-stage encoding step was critical for the generation of high-quality samples (as the DDPM component is agnostic to the nature of the input, and reproduces the quality of the reference data). While VAEs enable efficient image generation and data transfer, there is a known trade-off between image quality and diversity. Thus, further exploration in terms of balancing the quality and diversity is needed to optimize the data generation framework.

A recent study has also shown the capability of LDMs in generating high-quality brain images by utilising the UK Biobank dataset [18]. In comparison to the UK Biobank dataset, publicly available 3DE datasets are still very scarce, which complicates the training of such models. Our current model was trained with a comparatively small reference dataset (428 images). Subsequently, we observed that the synthetic data, while realistic, did not fully capture the complex noise characteristics of real echocardiograms. Other than the compression factor, our LDM did not utilize a discriminator model, which may be beneficial to further improve image quality.

Quantitatively, the FID score (13.7) indicated that the distribution of the synthetic images generated by DIFF·3 were similar to the training dataset, which was comparable to that obtained by the real MITEA test dataset (14.0). Since the calculation of FID relies on the feature extraction model, ImageNet, which was pre-trained on natural images rather than medical images with distinctly different features, our FID values cannot be benchmarked against those reported for natural 2D images.

In terms of image fidelity, DIFF·3 images produced a high IP score (0.888). Additionally, the moderate IR score (0.694) suggests that DIFF·3 is able to capture the majority of the target distribution. Compared to existing methods, IR scores achieved by synthetic data typically only range between 0.20–0.55, as demonstrated by Xu et al. in histopathology images [25].

Finally, diversity was measured using MS-SSIM, where the generated image samples are comparatively more diverse (0.710) with a lower MS-SSIM compared to the training dataset (0.781). However, the higher MS-SSIM of MITEA is in part attributed to the presence of scan-rescan images [28]. Meanwhile, MS-SSIM scores for HA-GAN were very high (0.99) which indicates the presence of duplicate synthetic images (as seen in 2), as a result of mode collapse due to the small amount of training data ($n = 428$). Consequently, DIFF·3 is more robust to small sample sizes.

As shown in Fig 3, having a large amount of synthetic data is required to fully span the data distribution. In this study, the addition of synthetic samples generated from the training data did not appear to improve segmentation network performance despite the addition of a substantial number of diverse synthetic samples. Previous studies have also found that the relative performance improvement owing to the addition of synthetic data is seen most prominently towards lower sample sizes of real data [5, 22]. This suggests that image quality (and not just diversity) becomes increasingly important for improving model generalizability for downstream tasks, particularly as the number of real samples increases.

4.1 Future Work

Despite the ability to generate synthetic data, DIFF·3 may still see improvement in terms of image quality. Currently, we rely on a 2D loss network, which creates subtle texture discontinuities between the image slices when reconstructed back into the 3D format. Exploring the use of 3D networks, such as MedicalNet [3] repurposed for perceptual tasks, may improve the fidelity of synthetic images. In addition, optimizing the compression factor and integrating a 3D discriminator model may further improve image quality, and thereby assist with downstream tasks such as segmentation.

5 Conclusion

By leveraging state-of-the-art LDMs, DIFF·3 provides an effective and efficient means of generating paired 3D echocardiograms and labels to supplement real patient data for deep learning applications.

Acknowledgements. We gratefully acknowledge the staff at the Centre for Advanced MRI at the University of Auckland for their expertise and assistance with the imaging components of this study.

Funding Statement. This study was funded by the Health Research Council of New Zealand (programme grant 17/608).

Code and data availability. Source code can be accessed in https://github.com/ EdwardFerdian/diff-3. Synthetic datasets are available upon request.

References

1. Akrout, M., et al.: Diffusion-based Data Augmentation for Skin Disease Classification: Impact Across Original Medical Datasets to Fully Synthetic Images (2023). arXiv:2301.04802
2. Alessandrini, M., et al.: A pipeline for the generation of realistic 3D synthetic echocardiographic sequences: methodology and open-access database. IEEE Trans. Medical Imaging **34**(7), 1436–1451 (2015). https://doi.org/10.1109/TMI.2015. 2396632
3. Alzubaidi, L.,et al.: MedNet: pre-trained convolutional neural network model for the medical imaging tasks. CoRR abs/2110.0 (2021) arXiv:2110.06512
4. Chambon, P., Bluethgen, C., Langlotz, C.P., Chaudhari, A.: Adapting Pretrained Vision-Language Foundational Models to Medical Imaging Domains (10 2022). arxiv:2210.04133
5. DuMont Schütte, A., et al.: Overcoming barriers to data sharing with medical image generation: a comprehensive evaluation. NPJ Digital Medicine **4**(1), 141 (2021). https://doi.org/10.1038/s41746-021-00507-3
6. Evain, E., Faraz, K., Grenier, T., Garcia, D., Craene, M.D., Bernard, O.: A pilot study on convolutional neural networks for motion estimation from ultrasound images. IEEE Trans. Ultrason. Ferroelectr. Freq. Control **67**(12), 2565–2573 (2020). https://doi.org/10.1109/TUFFC.2020.2976809
7. Gilbert, A., Marciniak, M., Rodero, C., Lamata, P., Samset, E., Mcleod, K.: Generating synthetic labeled data from existing anatomical models: an example with echocardiography segmentation. IEEE Trans. Med. Imaging **40**(10), 2783–2794 (10 2021). https://doi.org/10.1109/TMI.2021.3051806, https://ieeexplore. ieee.org/document/9324763/
8. Heusel, M., Ramsauer, H., Unterthiner, T., Nessler, B., Hochreiter, S.: GANs trained by a two time-scale update rule converge to a local nash equilibrium. In: Proceedings of the 31st International Conference on Neural Information Processing Systems, pp. 6629–6640. NIPS'17, Curran Associates Inc., Red Hook, NY, USA (2017)
9. Ho, J., Jain, A., Abbeel, P.: Denoising Diffusion Probabilistic Models. CoRR abs/2006.1 (2020). arXiv:2006.11239
10. Hong, S.: 3D-StyleGAN: a style-based generative adversarial network for generative modeling of three-dimensional medical images. In: Engelhardt, S., et al. (eds.) DGM4MICCAI/DALI -2021. LNCS, vol. 13003, pp. 24–34. Springer, Cham (2021). https://doi.org/10.1007/978-3-030-88210-5_3

11. Isensee, F., Jaeger, P.F., Kohl, S.A.A., Petersen, J., Maier-Hein, K.H.: NNU-Net: a self-configuring method for deep learning-based biomedical image segmentation. Nature Methods **18**(2), 203–211 (2021) https://doi.org/10.1038/s41592-020-01008-z

12. Jabri, A., Fleet, D.J., Chen, T.: Scalable Adaptive Computation for Iterative Generation. arXiv:2212.1 (2022)

13. Khader, F., et al.: Denoising diffusion probabilistic models for 3D medical image generation. Sci. Reports **13**(1), 7303 (2023). https://doi.org/10.1038/s41598-023-34341-2

14. Kynkäänniemi, T., Karras, T., Laine, S., Lehtinen, J., Aila, T.: Improved Precision and Recall Metric for Assessing Generative Models. In: NeurIPS 2019. arXiv (2019). arXiv:1904.06991

15. Lucidrains: Denoising Diffusion Probabilistic Model, in Pytorch (2020). https://github.com/lucidrains/denoising-diffusion-pytorch

16. Moghadam, P.A., et al.: A Morphology Focused Diffusion Probabilistic Model for Synthesis of Histopathology Images (2022). arXiv:2209.13167

17. Østivk, A., et al.: Myocardial function imaging in echocardiography using deep learning. IEEE Trans. Med. Imaging **40**(5), 1340–1351 (2021). https://doi.org/10.1109/TMI.2021.3054566

18. Pinaya, W.H.L., et al.: Brain imaging generation with latent diffusion models. In: Mukhopadhyay, A., Oksuz, I., Engelhardt, S., Zhu, D., Yuan, Y. (eds.) Deep Generative Models: Second MICCAI Workshop, DGM4MICCAI 2022, Held in Conjunction with MICCAI 2022, Singapore, September 22, 2022, Proceedings, pp. 117–126. Springer, Cham (2022). https://doi.org/10.1007/978-3-031-18576-2_12

19. Rombach, R., Blattmann, A., Lorenz, D., Esser, P., Ommer, B.: High-Resolution Image Synthesis with Latent Diffusion Models. CoRR abs/2112.1 (2021) arXiv:2112.10752

20. Song, J., Meng, C., Ermon, S.: Denoising Diffusion Implicit Models (2020). arXiv:2010.02502

21. Sun, L., Chen, J., Xu, Y., Gong, M., Yu, K., Batmanghelich, K.: Hierarchical amortized GAN for 3D high resolution medical image synthesis. IEEE J. Biomed. Health Inform. **26**(8), 3966–3975 (2022). https://doi.org/10.1109/JBHI.2022.3172976

22. Thambawita, V., et al.: SinGAN-Seg: Synthetic training data generation for medical image segmentation. PLOS ONE **17**(5), e0267976 (2022). https://doi.org/10.1371/journal.pone.0267976

23. Taigo, C., et al.: A data augmentation pipeline to generate synthetic labeled datasets of 3D echocardiography images using a GAN. IEEE Access **10**, 98803–98815 (2022). https://doi.org/10.1109/ACCESS.2022.3207177

24. Trabucco, B., Doherty, K., Gurinas, M., Salakhutdinov, R.: Effective Data Augmentation With Diffusion Models (2023). arXiv:2302.07944

25. Xu, X., Kapse, S., Gupta, R., Prasanna, P.: ViT-DAE: Transformer-driven Diffusion Autoencoder for Histopathology Image Analysis (2023)

26. youngjung: improved-precision-and-recall-metric-pytorch (2019). https://github.com/youngjung/improved-precision-and-recall-metric-pytorch

27. Zhang, R., Isola, P., Efros, A.A., Shechtman, E., Wang, O.: The Unreasonable Effectiveness of Deep Features as a Perceptual Metric (2018). arXiv:1801.03924

28. Zhao, D., et al.: MITEA: A dataset for machine learning segmentation of the left ventricle in 3D echocardiography using subject-specific labels from cardiac magnetic resonance imaging. Front. Cardiovasc. Med. **9** (2023). https://doi.org/10.3389/fcvm.2022.1016703
29. Zhou, Y., et al.: A framework for the generation of realistic synthetic cardiac ultrasound and magnetic resonance imaging sequences from the same virtual patients. IEEE Trans. Med. Imaging **37**(3), 741–754 (2018). https://doi.org/10.1109/TMI.2017.2708159

Author Index

J. M. Wolterink et al. (Eds.): SASHIMI 2023, LNCS 14288, pp. 141–142, 2023.
https://doi.org/10.1007/978-3-031-44689-4

Printed in the United States
by Baker & Taylor Publisher Services